"The level of honesty far surpasses anything a publisher has a right to expect."
—*Vanity Fair*

Ali MacGraw on Love Story:

"I guess I was a prime candidate for the rush of movie stardom: a walking time bomb of bottled-up ambition, ego, insecurity, and romanticism. Today I have the funny feeling that there was no escaping the combination of events that led up to *Love Story* . . . the tornado that picked me up and whirled me into space."

On Steve McQueen:

"The essential thing about Steve was that he exuded danger. You never knew what he was going to do or say next. . . . He had a kind of spell over me, with all of his macho swaggering. He liked to call me his Old Lady, a phrase I could live my whole life without hearing again."

On entering the Betty Ford Center:

"I checked in knowing I had made the right choice, but still stuck in what they call 'denial.' I did my best acting to portray a genteel lady with a severely broken heart— a little mixed up, perhaps, but basically just in need of a tune-up."

On her present-day life:

"I have learned a number of difficult lessons the hard way, because I guess I was always so sure that I had a better plan. . . . Today, like the child I remember as I walk in the Maine woods, I see *everything* as possible."

MOVING
PICTURES

Ali MacGraw

BANTAM BOOKS
New York · Toronto · London · Sydney · Auckland

MOVING PICTURES
A BANTAM BOOK

PRINTING HISTORY
Bantam hardcover edition published May 1991
Bantam paperback edition / April 1992

ISBN 0-553-29551-9

Published simultaneously in the United States and Canada

Bantam Books are published by Bantam Books, a division of Bantam
Doubleday Dell Publishing Group, Inc. Its trademark, consisting of the
words "Bantam Books" and the portrayal of a rooster, is Registered in
U.S. Patent and Trademark Office and in other countries. Marca Regis-
trada. Bantam Books, 666 Fifth Avenue, New York, New York 10103.

Printed in the United States of America

OPM   0   9   8   7   6   5   4   3

X X
4 Z
X X

and in loving memory
of my parents

Acknowledgments

It has taken me a number of years of stopping and starting to write this book, and there are certain people whose encouragement through all this time made it finally happen.

First, I want to thank my agent, the legendary Irving Lazar, for believing that I "had a book in me," as he put it, and for keeping after me until I got it done. My thanks to Richard Meryman for making me believe that I should—and could—write it myself, and for introducing me to the man without whom it most certainly would never have been done: David Outerbridge. I am grateful to David and to his wife, Lilias, for their support and generosity during all those weeks in their home in Belfast, Maine, where most of this book was written. In offering me their home and their friendship, they helped me to retrace my roots and finally to begin this journey.

My thanks, too, to the town of Belfast, which, like Malibu before it, provided me with a nurturing environment while I was living there. I am grateful to Kim Ryan in Maine for deciphering my illegible longhand and turning it into workable typewritten pages for David to organize. Thank you, Lori Hale in Los Angeles and Joe Pittman in New York, for performing the same role. And thanks to Alan Nevins for orchestrating so many details. I am also indebted to all the photographers who so generously allowed me the use of their photographs in this book.

I am grateful to so many friends who have been there for me during various times in my life; I think you know who you are. But writing this book turned out to be a far more stressful experience than I had ever imagined, and certain people were particularly supportive during this time. Thank you, Candice Bergen, Nicky Butler, José Eber, Arlie Manuel, Sue Mengers, Barbara Nessim, Michèle Parmiter, Byron Pedersen, Gilda Traylor, and Jeff Wald. And my thanks to Ann Sterling for finding me my first house.

Finally, I want to thank Linda Grey at Bantam for sticking with me months after this manuscript was due, believing that I had a story to tell and that I would finally deliver it. And my especial thanks to my editor, Beverly Lewis, who looked at the whole thing with a much-needed fresh eye long after I had grown dizzy with it, and with sensitivity and intelligence and remarkable patience helped to shape it into a real book.

I have been blessed to have certain "children" in my

life—beautiful grown-ups now. They have made my life richer: Terry and Chad McQueen, Lori and Tod Spangler, Robyn Westbrook, and Lauren Wild.

And finally, my deep gratitude to the hundreds, if not thousands of people whom I know only by their first names. Their unconditional acceptance and honesty have taught me how to live.

Author's Note

Out of respect for people's privacy, I have changed some of the names in this book.

At fifty.

I think I may be growing up at last.

I bought my first house today—not the eighteenth-century white clapboard farmhouse and barn I had always imagined, somewhere in New England. This one is a small adobe half-buried in the terra-cotta hills of Tesuque, New Mexico, as far away from my roots as are they from my temporary home, Los Angeles, where I have lived these many adventure-filled years. This little house is surrounded by pale silver shrubs and wild flowers whose names I have yet to learn, and the sky is a swiftly changing canvas of huge clouds chasing one another across a field of brilliant blue. At night I can touch the stars and the iridescent silver moon, and always I can breathe the clean, perfumed air. Like all good presents it came as a surprise, and like a child I catch myself smiling when I think about it.

It wasn't always this way. For so many years, in circumstances that seemed so perfect to the great invisible "them" out there, I existed as a kind of shadow woman. Part of me performed appropriately, and sometimes even brilliantly—much more so in life than I usually did on screen.

But there was another part of me that always, always felt that everything was happening to the shadow standing right next to me. All that attention. All that praise. All those fabulous times. The real me was there, too, with a fixed smile and a certain deceptive energy. But beneath the unconscious pose there was nearly always a dull ache in my heart. It was unfocused, but behind my eyes I was crying.

For a very long time I had no idea that there were two of me. Certainly I have been inordinately lucky this first half-century of my life, and often I was too distracted to take time to examine the anger and insecurity and raw fear that made me crave fixes to keep me from feeling. Prizes and lovers, tequila and chocolate. Attention and work. I needed them all to keep me from the edge of the deep black hole inside me.

Today everything is different, and some things are the same. I wake up less often with that terror in my selfish heart, that longing for a present—like a petulant child stamping her foot. Nowadays on my daily walks with my dogs I find myself saying out loud, over and over again, *Thank you.*

Thank you for that cobalt morning-glory vine, and thank you for the two sparrows playing in that tree.

Thank you for the fun my dogs are having in the leaves by the side of the road, and thank you, God, for the sweet-smelling breeze from the jasmine. Thank you for my friends. And for my animals. And for the miracle of my perfect child as he sets out on his own life at last. And for my sobriety.

And so every day, every moment brings its own lessons, its own treats, and I grow.

A WARM wind brings back memories of a long-ago day in Rome. It was 1967, and I had given up my part-time job as a fashion model and my rented apartment in New York to join my boyfriend in Rome for several months. He was an actor who had gotten a part in one of those spaghetti westerns so popular at the time, and I couldn't resist the chance to live in Italy. Life was all laughter and pasta and flirting in the Rome of the Sixties, and it was only a matter of time before we were collected, like every other new face in town, by the In Crowd. Night after night we joined dozens of charming strangers for long dinners alfresco on the Via Veneto and all-night dancing afterwards in the club of the moment.

One day we were invited to have lunch with the people who were working on Terry Southern's mad film *Barbarella*. We were picked up in a hideous gold Ferrari, and raced past the Colosseum and the Baths of Caracalla, to the Appian Way. It was very warm and the Roman traffic, especially at lunch hour, was as absurd as ever. But once on the rounded, worn stones of the Appian Way, we were in another land. It was suddenly very flat, and that ancient road, so narrow and full of history, cut through miles of fields. On either side there were pieces of the old Roman wall, broken and crowned with tufts of long, fawn-colored grass. There were fragments of statues—here a partial tombstone, a marble bust of a little child, a broken column—and there a fourth-century castle in ruins, with bricks that were bright pinkish brown, hot, dusty. We stopped for gas at a station whose walls were surfaced with chips of antique sculpture crushed into the cement.

The Vadims—Jane Fonda and Roger Vadim—had rented a fifteen-hundred-year-old villa, number 251 Appian Way. We drove down a country road, and suddenly we came upon the enormous old house. It was in the middle of wild fields, with surprising banks of papyrus looming up around it, their beige tops waving tall between the cypress. There were little white rock flowers spilling down some crumbling steps, and everywhere, Jane's animals. She had collected all sizes and shapes of baby dogs and tailless cats—one puppy looked more like a hedgehog than anything else. Small garden tables had been set with napkins and silver, and under a tree one table held a collection of bottles and little glasses of some bright-pink soft drink.

Inside, we all took plates of couscous from a huge buffet of saffron yellow. Vadim ate in the sun with the droll, pleasant French actor Serge Marquand. There were two girls, twins, slightly different but beautiful; they were in the film and were constantly buzzing about Vadim. In a shady corner David Hemmings was holding court, surrounded by three English girls. Jane Fonda came out of the house—an electric creature in orange pants and a ballet dancer shirt and a huge orange hat.

Suddenly everyone was in the far garden while some unidentified photographer took pictures. Jane called her animals, and one by one the entourage assembled.

It was wonderful to see people having such a marvelous time just being alive. In spite of the fact that they all had to work until three in the morning, they took a long, civilized lunch. I was not aware of any competition. Nobody was being a Movie Star. To me they were like children, playing in the grass.

Afterward we all drove to the unreal world of Dino de Laurentiis, where, ten minutes from the Appian Way, he had created a little white city, an entity of its own. Because *Barbarella* was science fiction, the lots were strewn with charred rocket hulls and plastic forms—toys in a multimillion-dollar game. At the same time, all the artists and technicians took their work very seriously. This was my first visit to a film set, and I marveled at the combination of hard work and fun, of fantasy and reality. The day was one unrecoverable moment, eternal, never to be experienced again.

A present, like every day.

I find it easiest to recapture moments like these when the sunlight falls a certain way, or in little things, like the marmalade cat that is tumbling about in my garden.

This is a story of shadows and shiny times, of my own life in the movies and out. It has many beginnings and endings and beginnings again—my life as a moving picture.

1

LOVE MEANS NEVER HAVING TO SAY YOU'RE SORRY

L ove means never having to say you're sorry.

With that absurd lie, millions of boxes of Kleenex were sold and a number of careers were launched. Including mine. There was absolutely nothing in my whole life experience to prepare me for the tornado that picked me up and whirled me into space when *Love Story* was released in December of 1970. Even the fact that I had already done one film and been very well received by the critics was nothing compared to the furor caused by *Love Story*.

It was not as though I had spent my childhood dreaming about Hollywood, or cutting out photographs of movie stars whose haircuts and clothing and celebrity I wanted to copy. In the small New England town where I grew up, I dreamed esoteric dreams of being a ballet dancer with Diaghilev's Ballets Russes or a member of the inner circle of the creative world of Paris in the Twenties. In every case my ego was alive and well, I must admit: in the first dream I was always the mistress of some member of the Imperial Family, dancing to rave reviews and decked to the hilt, like Mathilde Kschessinskaya, in real diamonds donated by my royal lover. And in the second dream I saw myself the very center of the bohemian life at the beginning of the century—the muse, perhaps, to Bonnard or Vuillard, the inspiration and companion to any number of the writers and musicians and artists who created and lived in a time that I found so terribly romantic. Anywhere but Bedford Village, New York. Anyone but Elizabeth Alice MacGraw, immaculate, conscientious little student and member of the community.

I guess I was a prime candidate for the rush of movie stardom: a walking time bomb of bottled-up ambition, ego, insecurity and romanticism. Today I have the funny feeling that there was no escaping the combination of events that led up to *Love Story* and to my marriage to Robert Evans, at that time the head of production of Paramount Studios and one of the most powerful and charming men in Hollywood. The two stories cannot be separated, because in many ways they were not only simultaneous but also made of the same surreal stuff. I see them both as one tremendous flash of light from the carbon arc of the dream machine; I look at them with affection and amazement, and I know that they were events that drastically altered my life.

There were several coincidences in the unfolding of my involvement with *Love Story* and with Robert Evans. In the first place, I had actually met Bob before—years before, when I was between my final years in college, trying to make a living as a college model. I had posed for an advertisement for some kind of fake fur coat in the broiling August sun one afternoon in New York City's Sutton Place. My agent, the formidable Eileen Ford, informed me that a Robert Evans had seen me posing for the picture and would like to invite me to lunch. I had not only never met Robert Evans, I didn't read the tabloids and gossip columns and had no way of knowing that he was considered one of the great ladies' men of his time; I lived too sheltered a life. But as I stood at the telephone in the middle of our little living room, with no privacy whatever, I figured I might just as well meet this man, since Eileen Ford was urging me and she insisted that he was nice. At least I would have a good lunch on my way to another fruitless model's audition.

I met Mr. Evans at some then-fashionable lunch spot, where all I can remember is the kind of Las Vegas–like showgirls who sat at the bar, and the astonishing fact that after ordering me ground steak and carrots and peas, he proceeded to spend the entire time on not one but two telephones, which were brought to the table. After lunch he politely offered to have a taxi take me to my next appointment; that saved me from my usual complication of cross-town bus connections. But when he got out at the Seventh Avenue address of the women's clothing business that he ran very successfully with his brother Charles, he neglected to pay the fare. It stuck in my memory, this peculiar meeting; nor shall I ever forget his remark as I stretched out my legs on the jump seat of the Yellow Cab: "Those are the ugliest shoes I have ever seen," he said of the brand-new pair of Capezios I had just bought wholesale at the warehouse. I was crushed; they were my only fancy shoes.

I was obviously not a hit as a date, because I didn't see Robert Evans again for almost a decade, by which time he and his brother had sold Evan-Picone for a lot of money and gone into separate businesses. Bob had become first a producer and then head of production for Paramount. It was he who had made the final decision to cast me as Brenda in my first real movie, *Goodbye, Columbus*. And it was he who would oversee the entire state-of-the-art hype surrounding that experience called *Love Story*.

Another funny coincidence was that when my agent first sent me the script for *Love Story*, I did not particularly register the name of the author. I read the script once, fast, and cried, and then I read it a second time to be sure that I had been paying attention. All of a sudden I realized that Erich Segal was in fact someone I had known in college: when I was at Wellesley, he was at Harvard, several years ahead of me, and we had actually been in my one and only play at Wellesley together. It was Shakespeare's *All's Well That Ends Well*. The lovers were played by me and the Harvard student who was my future husband, and Erich played the villain. Who knew that he would go on to become an important classics scholar and the author of a little book that would be a bestseller in every language in the world?

The events that led to my playing the role of Jennifer Cavilleri in *Love Story* are fairly straightforward—it was literally the only script offered to me that I liked, after my debut in *Goodbye, Columbus*. Paramount had signed me to a three-picture deal in exchange for putting a total unknown into her first feature, and as the months went by and one awful script after another was sent to me in New York, I was terrified that I was going to be forced to do something I loathed. When my agent sent me the script for *Love Story*, it came with an offer from another studio of $120,000 for the "girl in *Goodbye, Columbus*"— an unheard-of amount of money for me. But I had liked working at Paramount, and I trusted them to make the best picture possible; I asked them if I could do *Love Story* as my second contract film and they agreed. My salary was $20,000—still an absolute fortune to me.

From the second I was signed to do the film, I was excited. Everything was still very fresh in my brief experience of movie-making, and I was thrilled to be doing a project I liked. I even had the idiotic delusion that I was a bit in control, because Bob Evans called to request that I fly out to California for the day to see the as-yet-unreleased film *Popi* and to meet its director, Arthur Hiller, whom he said he was considering for *Love Story*. That shows how naïve I was: of course Arthur had already been signed, because he was—and is—tremendously in demand, and we were lucky to get him. My emergency trip to Beverly Hills and the screening room of Bob Evans was probably little more than a high-powered seduction scene. It sure worked.

I had been living with a young actor, and it had been an extremely volatile, difficult relationship. He had spent the summer in Los Angeles trying to find work, and it was about the time of the Manson murders. Hollywood seemed to me a distant and sinister place as I boarded that plane to "meet the director" for one night. My boyfriend had just returned to New York the evening before, and we had had no time to get reacquainted—ships passing in the night.

When the studio limousine met me at the airport I was carrying just one small change of clothing and my return ticket to New York for the next day. It all felt like a great rush, First Class Fun. When I arrived at the Evans house, I was speechless at the opulence of it. I had never experienced anything like it: the Regency grandeur (Beverly Hills version); the cobalt-tiled swimming pool that separated the house from the screening room, each building candlelit and warmed by its own fireplace; the music piped everywhere; the enormous sycamore trees and gardens filled with roses and kumquats and lemons and thousands of cutting flowers.

I did not have time to draw a full breath before I was met at the door by the houseman, David Gilruth. Even as he handed me the first of God knows how many glasses of champagne, I liked him immediately. He seemed kind and real, less intimidating than the rest of the scene.

Looking back, I guess those twenty-four hours were one of the great drunks of my life: I remember sleeping through the dinner, which was brought on trays to the projection room where we were to watch *Popi*. I also slept through the film, and woke only long enough to throw myself fully clothed, high heels and all, into the swimming pool. I remember, too, thinking that I was behaving just as Zelda Fitzgerald, one of my earlier idols, might have done. I spent the night in the master bedroom of that house. And I never left.

Conveniently, I caught a stomach flu—or was it a tremendous hangover?—that lasted for three or four days, during which time David Gilruth brought me my meals on a tray and told me outrageous stories that made me laugh.

I called my boyfriend in New York and told him that inasmuch as we had not seen each other all summer anyway, and things had not been going that well, I wanted to end our relationship then and there. Not surprisingly, he figured out that I wanted to stay with Bob. I don't know that I behaved with any sensitivity, but I do know that I felt tremendous relief. Somewhere inside me I felt that at last I was safe, that I would no longer have to be the one who took care of everybody. Someone wanted to take care of me.

No one had ever been as generous to me as Bob. I had never seen the likes of how he lived—the luxury of it. It did not seem real to me, not then, not ever. But it was thrilling and flattering and spoiling, the prelude to the blur that would be my life as a movie star. From the dinner-party guest lists of everyone I had ever heard of, to the thirty-two telephones scattered around the house, to the first-class style of every single thing we did, my life moved in a dizzying spiral. I had landed on another planet.

With no clothes. One of the first things Bob did, in his Jay Gatsby way, was to order me special trousers designed by Holly Harp: twelve at a time, in different colors and fabrics. He joked that my clothes took up only two and a half feet in one of his closets. The rest of the twenty-by-twenty-foot mirrored dressing room was for his clothes. He called me "my little hippie"—and even so, *Women's Wear Daily* constantly noted what I was wearing and Eleanor Lambert put me on her best-dressed list the year that *Love Story* came out.

In the early weeks of our relationship we were gossiped about and photographed everywhere we went. I wore headbands then, a kind of token hippie touch from a squeaky-clean spirit of the 1960s, too scared to try LSD but crazy about ethnic clothes and peace rallies. Every other photograph from that time shows me in my headband of the moment—a costume collector somehow launched uncomfortably and tenuously into the limelight. It all moved so fast that I could only go with it and enjoy it. Somehow, in the space of the few months since *Goodbye, Columbus* had made me a "promising new face" in the movies, I had managed to be swept up in the quintessential Hollywood scene.

Because production had begun on *Love Story,* Bob and I were both caught up in the busy-ness of that project, and every moment was a whirlwind. My work consisted of the usual things, like having a wardrobe fitted and memorizing my part, but one added job was testing with all the gifted actors who were being considered for the part of Oliver. A number of them—including Jon Voight, Beau Bridges, Michael Douglas, and Michael Sarrazin—had turned it down, but there were plenty of wonderful ones who had not. I had to kiss them all—Christopher Walken and Ken Howard and David Birney, among others. (Not a bad job, I must say!) But the part went, of course, to Ryan O'Neal, at the very last minute, and it is impossible to think of anyone but Ryan playing that role. He was already a huge television star from the soap opera *Peyton Place; Love Story* earned Ryan an Academy Award nomination and the status of movie star.

I loved working with him; he was sexy and sensitive, surly and funny, all things, all of the time. He and Arthur

Hiller made all of us laugh from morning to night, and like *Goodbye, Columbus* before it, *Love Story* gave me the mistaken feeling that making a film was a sweet ensemble experience. From the first time that Ryan and Arthur and I met to rehearse in an apartment overlooking Central Park in New York, I felt that I was part of something special; I think we all did. And I think that as poorly trained as I was as an actress, my sad demeanor at the end of that movie came as much from my knowing that it would end soon as from any proper actor's preparation for Jenny's death scene.

Bob, in the meanwhile, had come up with a brilliant idea: to have Erich Segal write a book from his screenplay, which Harper & Row released as a kind of seasonal throwaway on Valentine's Day of 1970. To everyone's amazement the novel became an overnight bestseller. By the time the movie was released the following Christmas, *Love Story* was at the top of the bestseller lists. It was a clever bit of merchandising: the film was assured a huge opening and anticipated in countries all over the world.

With the Hollywood machine going a million miles an hour to create a hit, Bob and I began living together in his Beverly Hills mansion. I had given up my little apartment on New York's Upper West Side and, with considerable trepidation, packed up my books and clothes and Scottie dog to move from the East Coast for the first time. I shall never forget how I felt as the limousine pulled away from Manhattan, that wonderful skyline receding right along with my sense of reality. Where was I going? What would my life be like? Who would be my friends? As the light of the late-day sun caught the facets of the extravagant sapphire engagement ring

Bob had given me, I had very mixed feelings. I felt both a sense of great adventure and a simultaneous terror at being uprooted from everything I knew. But I also felt I was in safe hands with Bob, and after twenty-odd years of tremendous ups and downs and drama, our close enduring friendship tells me that I was right.

Life for the young Hollywood couple was nonstop glamour. So many times I read clippings about where we had eaten or how I had dressed or who had sat next to us in the theater, and wondered whom they were writing about. Many of our evenings were spent in the projection room, where Bob's already long days continued well past midnight. He loved his work, and his work was the movies. With the exception of our son, Josh, there has probably never been anything or anyone to capture Bob's heart the way the movies always have. Night after night we sat in our bathrobes in that room, watching cut number twenty-one of a film that needed tremendous postproduction help from Bob and his editor. I usually fell asleep after the first few viewings, but Bob had an unbelievable memory for detail and could always recall just which frame of which shot would make a sequence play better. It's a real art, and Bob is as good at it as anyone.

But his work (and the infernal attendant telephone) did consume his life, seven days a week, every week of the year. Nowadays I wonder if that is not the common denominator among all the successful Hollywood moguls, but back then I came to miss conversations and gatherings that had to do with something other than The Business. It scared me that it was possible for every waking hour of work or pleasure to be centered around the same subject, but I think that is how it really is.

In the early months of our relationship I spent my time trying to figure out how to fit into the Evans household. At first I was like any number of girlfriends who had stayed at Bob's house; I spent my time doing brand-new lazy things, like sitting in the sun or shopping—that Beverly Hills profession—or fooling with the garden. For a while I loved the laziness of this life: we were busy every evening, either with a dinner party or in the projection room, and the days were a delicious vacation for me in Never-Never Land. Bob had a maid who'd been with him for a long time, a large woman who was fiercely loyal to her employer and watched over him and his house like a guard dog. At first she went out of her way to be nice to me—all smiles and solicitude. But when it finally dawned on her that I might be in the house to stay, she turned on me, making it very plain that she was the woman of the house and that I was dispensable. As I had never really had anyone work for me until then, I had no idea how to handle the situation. Bob was away all day at the office, and I tiptoed around the perfectly polished rooms, enduring her glares and occasional remarks like "What are you doing in *my* kitchen?"

Just before the actual filming of *Love Story* began in the autumn of 1969, Bob asked me to marry him. As fast as things had moved, it felt like what I wanted, and I called my parents to tell them how happy I was. The wedding had to be soon, because I was leaving for Boston to begin work. For some reason we decided to have an invisible ceremony with a justice of the peace in Riverside, California, one of the ugliest spots in America, but right between Beverly Hills and Palm Springs, where we would at least be able to spend the weekend. It was all arranged with incredible secrecy by the publicity department at Paramount—and then announced by them to every press outlet in the world. It was odd, I must say. The good part was that my friend Peggy Morrison, who had worked with me during the early days in New York, came down from Big Sur to be my witness. Her presence was a big support for me.

Bob's best man was his brother and closest friend, Charles, who came from New York to spend that weekend with us. Charles, Peggy, David Gilruth, and the housekeeper joined Bob and me in a nondescript little room in the Riverside town hall for the fastest wedding service on record. Then we drove the hour to Palm Springs and a friend's house to spend the short weekend before *Love Story* began.

I have a curious memory of that Saturday: I was in the swimming pool, watching the water and light play on my engagement ring. For some reason I grew terribly sad and frightened, and I began to cry. When Bob asked me what the matter was, I told him I knew he had been with every beautiful woman in the world, and I was sure he wouldn't be faithful to me. He said, very sternly, "If you continue to dwell on your worst fears, they will probably come true, so I think you had better get hold of yourself now." It chilled me, but I knew he was right. Bob was such a legendary ladies' man for his whole life that I was terrified I wouldn't measure up to his need to be with a beautiful, sexy woman. I worried about that a lot, and maybe it wasn't so stupid after all. In a book published much later he told our friend David Brown that he really did not think he could ever be faithful to anyone—not even me. I kept that fear deep inside me and used it to rationalize the infidelity I began with Steve McQueen, a kind of sick logic about "doing it before it was done to me." If I look honestly at the situation, I have to see how little trust I had in Bob or any other man, for reasons that would become more apparent as I began to dig into my childhood.

But that was later. The overriding feeling of the early days of my marriage to Bob was that we were in love, two highly successful people in a business that idolizes winners (and, as I would later find out, scorns people whose winning streaks have taken a detour). We apparently looked good enough together that people in Hollywood seemed to love the idea of us as a couple, part of the ultimate fantasy of the dream machine.

It was fun to be there, in many ways: after a lifetime of craving approval, I was getting it on all sides. I was flattered constantly by everyone—for my work, my clothes, my so-called style—and I was loved and protected by a man who knew how to make me feel more special than I had ever felt in my life. I had no time to think, or worry, or indulge in any kind of introspection. I was living an all-stops-out glamorous, celebrated life, and I could hardly believe it was happening to me.

Was I happy? I think so. I must have been. But a tiny corner of me was beginning to wonder if I hadn't gotten a little carried away with this rarefied new life, if I had not, perhaps, lost some of my integrity. I was aware that I was so crazy about being popular that I would go to outrageous lengths to be sure that every single person in a room liked me, no matter what I really thought of them. I was perceived as Miss Hollywood Charm; it was not required of me either—I just decided that I needed to behave that way.

Bob was much truer to himself, and though he was a master manipulator when it came to deals and publicity, he never made up stories about who he was or what he liked. He had a self-deprecating sense of humor, and he was never more charming than when he told a tale at his own expense. He had a practically photographic memory, and he could go on and on for hours about the great life of Hollywood in the Fifties, which is when he came in, as an actor. He had that rarest of all qualities out in Lotusland: good manners. When my parents came to visit us in our imposing house, he made them feel special and at home. He had grace and charm to spare.

I say "had" only because I am remembering a particular moment in our now twenty-one-year friendship. But these qualities are intrinsic to Bob, as are some of the maddening ones that caused trouble for him during a decade of obsessive behavior and bad judgment. I think that the Hollywood game of Brass Ring breeds a kind of madness and insecurity in all of us, and many of us have crashed and burned at least once in the course of it. Bob is a survivor with style; he is also a gambler who lives to play high stakes, and I have no doubt that he will win.

The actual filming of *Love Story* seemed to pass by in a flash. I loved the fact that we were staying near Cambridge, because it brought back all the good memories of my time in college. We were there in the fall, which is my favorite time of year, particularly in New England. I remember the experience of making that film as pure fun. Much of the work was done in New York City, which I have always considered home. I was able to see a lot of my parents and certain old friends, so in many ways, I did not feel that I had really moved away. That added to the unreal quality of making *Love Story*—that temporary illusion I always have when I am doing a movie, that wherever I am working is home.

When the filming ended, a period of unreality truly began for me. I always felt, at best, a welcome visitor in Los Angeles. Idiotically, I had never learned to drive, so there I was at nearly thirty years old, waiting meekly for a ride into town to do various errands or, better yet, walking the two miles. In that particular suburb you are cruised as a vagrant if you are seen walking for any length of time on the sidewalks. I had my share of questioning by the local security patrols, but in fact I did not actually learn to drive for several more years. It was David who saved me from feeling a total captive; he took me along on his errands and on sightseeing junkets. Still, I felt dumb and outcast.

It was a huge change for me to go from being a full-time working girl to a rather rich lady of leisure. As many nice people as I met during our endless evenings of entertaining, I really had no one to replace my New York friends. For the most part, I entertained myself in the garden or with my drawing and reading, and waited until the evening for company or a social life. And it was all right; it was like an extended holiday, I suppose.

As the postproduction continued on *Love Story*, Bob worked harder and harder on the film, which some insiders thought was going to be a surprise big hit. He commissioned a musical score, first from Burt Bacharach, then from Jimmy Webb, but when they both turned out to be somehow not quite right, he got in touch with the

French composer Francis Lai. Claude Lelouch's *A Man and a Woman* was the big romantic hit of the moment, and one of the reasons was certainly Francis Lai's music. When Francis said that he was too exhausted to work on another score over that summer of 1970, Bob flew to Paris to try to persuade him otherwise. His friend Alain Delon had a little dinner for us in his apartment, and afterward Francis and all the guests watched a rough cut of *Love Story*—with the music from *A Man and a Woman* temporarily set in. Luckily, everyone cried in all the predictable places, and Francis agreed to score the film from his vacation home high above the French Riviera.

At the same time, Bob dropped a bomb on me when he came home from the editing room to tell me that as far as he was concerned, the picture was unreleasable: too much talk. He sent Arthur Hiller and Ryan and me, along with the producer and cinematographer, back to Boston in the fall of 1970, where, with no permits and no extra union assistance, we sneaked all the dialogue-free footage that makes up the connective tissue of the film. Over it was laid the music that won Francis Lai the Academy Award, and to this day I think that the mega-success of *Love Story* was determined by those two decisions.

For Paramount, Bob had to travel to Europe often during the year. Whether we were in London or Paris or Rome there were always interesting film people he had to see. While those days were a bit frenzied and all-consumed by The Movies, they were still exhilarating. My mind and my eyes were stretched by my adventures in Europe. Afterward, Los Angeles was never a big enough world for me.

In early summer of 1970, Bob and I discovered we were going to have a baby, and although our schedule was as hectic as ever, I had never felt better in my life. I had never really thought much one way or the other about having children; I assumed that I would have some one day, but when it happened that "one day" was soon, I was thrilled, and so was Bob. In a typical gesture, he had thousands of tulip bulbs planted in our front yard, so that one of my favorite flowers would be in bloom when the baby came. (Ironically, because I was marooned in New York during the final months of my pregnancy, all two thousand of them came up, bloomed, and wilted without my ever seeing them that year.)

Love Story opened December 16, 1970, at the Loews Theatre on Broadway in New York City. It was already a much anticipated picture, because the inside word was that it was good. There was a big charity opening, to which people like Henry Kissinger and Ted Kennedy were invited, along with every celebrity on the East Coast. The preceding week was crammed with interviews and appearances, including the Ed Sullivan show, on which I appeared, exceedingly pregnant, in a Syrian coat and a knitted hat and tribal jewelry—reciting the Desiderata, of all things. (I mean, what else was I qualified to do? Sing "Home on the Range"?) I was photographed for virtually every magazine, often for the cover, and accorded that kind of heat and attention that is a sure sign of movie stardom, at least for the moment. It was pretty heady stuff.

The night of the opening I was sitting on the floor of our hotel suite, wrapping presents. Suddenly I realized that I was sitting in a pool of blood. Terrified, Bob called our doctor. Of course, the doctor wanted me to cancel my evening, but he settled on giving me an injection of some sort with my promise that I would go straight from the premiere to the hospital and remain there for two weeks. I don't know what he gave me, but I do not remember much about that evening except for the sound of lots of people sniffling and crying. As I drove off to the peace and quiet of the hospital, I realized two things: that our picture was a hit, and that I was luckier than anyone I knew not to have lost the baby by my idiotic decision to stay a few extra hours in the stress and craziness of that evening. Gratefully, I checked into a hospital room where the telephone had been shut off, and I stayed there through Christmas, visited only by my parents and Bob's brother and sister and their families.

I was released from the hospital after two weeks but was advised not to fly for the duration of my pregnancy. Bob had returned to Los Angeles to work on *The Godfather*, and I was happily ensconced in the Sherry Netherland Hotel to wait until the baby was born. Pleased to be close to my family and my friends, I spent a lazy time, mostly in our suite, and looked forward to Bob's returning in a few weeks.

One night an old friend, Andrea Eastman, came by for supper, which was our ritual room-service salad and white wine. She brought along a bottle of curry powder, as we had both decided that the hotel salad dressing left a lot to be desired. After several glasses of wine and a lot of curry and laughter, I suddenly noticed that I was soaking wet, and I asked Andrea—who had never had a baby either—if she thought my water might have broken, six weeks early. With all the authority of a non-parent, she assured me that it could not have, and we laughed and carried on until past midnight, when she had to go to the airport to meet her boyfriend. By the time she left I was having hideous cramps, and I figured that I had best go to the hospital. But with whom? The elevator man? Bob's brother Charles? What if it was a false alarm and I disturbed him at two o'clock in the morning for nothing? I tried to bore myself to sleep with a ponderous book, but to no avail, and I finally did rouse poor Charles out of a sound sleep to take me to the hospital. He has always been there for his family, and this time was no exception.

Joshua was born late the following morning, on January 16, 1971, more than a month early and exactly one month after the day *Love Story* opened. I had planned to have him naturally, but because of my hemorrhage in December, I had to have some medication. As I fell into a druggy sleep at the end of the uncomfortable ordeal that women have always known better than to tell their girlfriends about, I got my first sight of Josh. He was in a basket, I guess, with his little feet poking out at the end. Hallucinating like mad, I looked at him and sighed, "Oh—that is my baby! Look at those big feet. And it's a boy—he's wrapped in a blue sheet." And then I was out. I may have imagined this whole scenario, but I do know that no event ever in my life has been so profound, so joyful, so moving. I fell in love as I never have before or since.

Charles had called Bob at home in Beverly Hills, and he caught the first plane out that morning. I was terribly sad for him that he had missed the actual birth, but it had come so unexpectedly that there was no avoiding it. And although, like so many men, he regarded a baby as a somewhat mysterious and possibly breakable creature,

Bob, too, discovered the person who would become his best friend in life.

The birth of Joshua only added more frenzy to the externals of our life, because it was one more piece of the movie star puzzle for columnists and paparazzi. If the nanny was taking the baby for a ride in Central Park, sooner or later some crazed photographer would leap out from behind a tree to take his picture. Ron Galella and company even chased me into the elevator at our hotel. Somehow, everywhere any of us went there was a photographer waiting. It was unnerving, and I knew I was powerless to control it. No one had warned me that this ride called Celebrity is at a thousand miles an hour; once it starts, you can't jump off. It would be easier when we got back home to the safety of our gated garden and house.

But before we could settle down, there were two more important premieres for *Love Story*. The first one was for the Queen Mother's favorite charity in London, a Royal Command Performance at which we would be introduced to Her Gracious Majesty. Several weeks later Madame Pompidou would host a screening and a gala party for her favorite charity, in Paris.

I was exhausted right after Josh was born, but I needed to be well-dressed and pulled together for the press coverage in those two countries. I called Halston and asked if I could come up to his salon and buy some postpregnancy clothes. We chose wonderful, simple things, and I went off on this press tour packed as minimally as possible with one dress for each occasion.

UNFORTUNATELY, I had caught the flu in New York, and by the time I arrived in London I was so dizzy and feverish that I could barely stand up. Bob and I checked into the Connaught on the afternoon of the premiere, just in time to send my dress out to be pressed and to have my hair done. There was one other preparation: every big city seems to have a doctor on call whose medicine bag contains a remedy for every imaginable emergency. We phoned the one in London, and he quickly appeared at our hotel, a vision in tie and tails, his doctor bag a cascading pull-out of any drug you could possibly want. In two seconds his shot of God-only-knows-what pulled me through my flu and into euphoria. I felt wonderful, ready to meet the Queen Mother and do the extravagant curtsy I had been practicing in the bathroom.

There was just one little problem: I couldn't figure out which way to put on my simple silk jersey T-shirt dress. All set to go, flying high, I put that dress on several different ways, and no matter how I turned it, it hung unevenly and one of my breasts poked out. Not exactly the Command Performance look, so, ranting under my breath about both Halston and the hotel's ancient valet and his steam iron, I threw on the only other black-tie outfit I had brought with me, which happened to be trousers—hardly appropriate for the occasion.

Before the screening of the film, the gang from *Love Story* were joined by other American actors working in London at the time. We were all placed in a semicircle to be formally introduced to the Queen Mother. She was attired in a lemon-yellow Martha Washington–cake dress and crown jewels, a dear-looking lady, I must say. She was joined by her younger daughter, Princess Margaret, and as each of our names was announced, we made a deep bow or curtsy. As Princess Margaret passed by me I could have sworn I heard her say, "My husband saw your film in New York last week and didn't particularly care for it." "Thank you, ma'am," deep curtsy. We were all dumbfounded to realize later that she had managed to make that same comment to everyone in the receiving line who was connected with the film.

Love Story was an overnight blockbuster in London, and we returned to New York tired but very proud. There was just one bit of business to attend to: why had Halston's expensive dress disintegrated with one little stroke of the iron? Bob was livid, and barely controlling himself, he demanded that Halston see what a disgrace his costume had been.

Coolly, Halston asked that I come up to his salon and try on the offending dress, in front of him and his two super-blasé assistants, all of them posing with long cigarette holders. I put on the dress for this audience; out popped the dreaded breast again. "See, Halston? I mean, this is so unfortunate," I said.

Ever so patronizingly, he suggested that I turn the dress around, to the only aperture I hadn't put my head through in London. It was perfect. I couldn't help but wonder exactly what drug that Doctor Feelgood had given me back there at the Connaught. I felt like an idiot.

Luckily, I hadn't said a word to anyone in the press about the incident, and the next day I sent Halston twelve dozen tulips for the opening of his collection. The press did note the accompanying card, which read—what else?—"Love Means Never Having to Say You're Sorry."

Over the twenty years since *Love Story* I have thought

about the effect it had on my life. I see it as mostly wonderful: the film work, the good reviews, the Oscar nomination, the Golden Globe award, the well-wishing fans, even the treats that come with pop stardom. I have also come to realize that poor reviews of later work are not the whole truth about my acting, any more than the over-the-top, gushy ones were in the early days. Somewhere in the middle lies the truth about my credibility as an actress. All in all, I am blessed to have been part of that rare gift for any performer: a huge hit.

As far as my relationship with Bob goes, I think we would probably both have to say that the months centered around the making and release of *Love Story* marked a high point for us. We were in such a rarefied atmosphere in those days—winners, each, for a moment and living a life together that had little time for anything but applause and success.

I look back on those several stardusted years we had together with a kind of amazement and tremendous gratitude. And always I will remember the New Year's Eve just before Josh was born. Bob and I were walking down Fifth Avenue for a little celebration dinner with my agent, Sue Mengers, and her husband. It was snowing gently. In the streetlamp-lit flurry of the snow I could see all the way across 59th Street, where, high up on the Gulf & Western Building, were the words LOVE STORY: Bob's monster hit for Paramount in 1970–'71 and my catapult into stardom.

Interlude

Maine, *February 1990*

I am curled up in a big wing chair in the library of a comfortable farmhouse in Belfast, Maine, writing this book. There is a fire burning for me, and endless pots of smoky Lapsang Soochong tea to drink. I am content to stay indoors and write, safely wrapped up in this cocoon that reminds me of nothing so much as the best parts of my childhood.

It is winter today: no more early spring slush to spoil the pristine whiteness of the snow in the woods. Today the sun is out, after a humid, leaden-gray sky yesterday, and the temperature has dropped forty degrees, to below zero. Everywhere it is shining and sparkling.

I am so content and peaceful here. It is as though I have been rescued from my off-the-track life in still-alien California. Strange, but after twenty years in Los Angeles, I still don't belong—part of me still cannot breathe. This book could never have been written there. I have to be back in New England, with my heart-roots.

It is as if I had lived the extended life of a visiting stranger all these years, pushing myself further and further from my own center.

I chose some odd books to bring here, in case I am lucky enough to have time to read at the end of the day: Jack London, my new favorite writer, and Anne Morrow Lindbergh's *Gift from the Sea,* which I may have read bits of a long time ago. What a wonderful guide. I read it last night, and it reminded me that whatever we call it— "meditation," or quiet, alone time—each of us needs a period of absorbed stillness each day. Slowly I am giving myself permission to find that so-called meditation my own way.

I love the reassuring sounds of a house in the country in winter: the crackle of an all-day fire—for warmth, not mood—the howl of the wind against the house, the sudden sighs of the golden retriever as he settles himself on the down-filled couch and hand-embroidered pillow, his sweet brown eyes taking in the stranger and finding her okay. There is a slim version of my cat Dudley living here. He spent the morning curled up on my lap and on the volume I am trying to use as a desk. Finally he had to go off and curl up under a huge geranium that is finding a new and wonderful winter life blooming in the sunny window. Blue, a border collie, slept on my bed last night, splaying herself diagonally across three quarters of the bed. I loved it. It was a sign of approval, I think. And as if that weren't enough to keep me warm these cold nights, I had a special visitor in the middle of the night: the shiny, svelte black cat, who climbed under the covers for warming.

I feel utterly at home.

The danger is that I will fatten up here. I remember how irresistible it was just to nibble and drink tea all day and all night when I went home to Bedford Village as a grown-up. I see clearly today how those visits were more than just a checkup on my aging parents; they were a "fix" for me. Somewhere deep inside of me I could pretend to be partly child again—someone with parents, a family. I do not have a real family now except for Joshua. I have made friends my family.

But today I am wallowing in the marvels of being almost alone in this very special place. I gleefully turned off my answering machine when I left home and rushed to the airport early, running to be certain nothing would detain me from leaving. Almost nobody can find me. And so I can work and, in my own way perhaps, through this book, try to find out who I am again. There is no doubt in my mind that I shall, and soon.

My sense-memory of this part of the world is intense. Even though I am miles from Bedford Village, New York, it feels the same. There, too, winter was a blanket of nearly virgin snow, speckled with the ever-changing paw prints of the little creatures of the forest. Outside our window, as here, was a special tree festooned with bird feeders full of sunflower seeds, and belted with wire collars of suet for the blue jays. The ground beneath was always a litter of sunflower hulls and crumbled stale bread, a chessboard for the bird-game of Which Species Get the Most to Eat. I never tired of watching the special secret order of eating observed by the fat little chickadees, splendid blue jays, and woodpeckers. My sense of it was that there might have been some real rules at the beginning of winter, but by early February—now—it was every bird for himself.

What I love about this kind of country is the fundamental stillness; even the occasional car driving by on the local tar road has a different sound. In Los Angeles there is not even a minute without the sound and stench of an automobile. It is taken-for-granted background clamor, anesthetizing at first, and ultimately infuriating.

Here, when it snows in the forest, you can hear the delicate sound of each flake as it falls, and the crisp air hums with its own odd, electrical charge. The fire flaps in the fireplace, the logs occasionally grunting and turning over in a flurry of sparks. Even the sounds of the mechanical things in the house are somehow soothing. Each hour that goes by catapults me deeper and deeper into another time and another person.

As I sit here in this cozy home in Maine, I realize that I get to choose how I want to see and interpret and live every remaining moment of my life, and so I pay attention.

2

HELLO, LIFE
GOODBYE, COLUMBUS
(OR WAS IT THE
OTHER WAY AROUND?)

On January 11, 1971, *Time* magazine put me on its cover for a story called "The Return to Romance." In an interview that surpassed an FBI cross-examination in its depth, I told them my version of the story of my life, and I certainly designed it to fit the title of the article. When I reread it now, I am amazed at the gentle invention I made of my childhood in a quaint little town called Bedford Village, an hour north of Manhattan, on the border between Westchester County and Connecticut. "My parents were artists," I said, and "in the winter my brother and I sat in front of the fireplace and talked with my father, surrounded by books. We were very, very loved."

Parts of this story were true: certainly we were loved, and certainly there were a lot of books in the house. My parents worked as free-lance commercial artists, and they were educated, even intellectuals. But what was missing from my rhapsody about my childhood was the fact that we were living in a house where something was terribly off balance. I think back to those days and know now that there was an atmosphere of fear and hidden tension, always.

Now I understand what it was: there was never a moment when my brother and I could be sure that my father would not lose control of his terrifying temper. To this day I am nearly faint when I see an adult raise his (or her) hand to a child. It brings back the most terrible memories of my childhood, when, with no rational prov-ocation, my father would stalk one of us for what was called in our house a "spanking." My brother was by far the more persecuted of the two of us, but I had my share of those spankings, and I was literally sick to my stomach with fear from as far back as I can remember. For years I suffered from acute insomnia and a spastic colon. On many occasions the atmosphere was anything but tran-quil and nourishing.

Daddy was left fatherless at a very early age, separated from his brothers and sisters at six and sent to an or-phanage. He never forgave his real parents for destroying his childhood, and until the day he died he never dis-cussed the details of his tragedy with anyone. The little fragments of information I learned after his death did little more than enhance the lifelong mystery that was Daddy's creation of himself.

At a time when psychoanalysis and therapy were con-sidered self-indulgent, he had no way to deal with the pain but to drink. When my mother was pregnant with me, she persuaded him to stop, and to his credit, he did.

But he lived the next twenty-one years of his life in white-knuckle rage, all the pain and loneliness festering inside while his pride kept him from revealing his vulnerability to any of us. When I think about it now, my heart breaks for the seventy-odd years of pain he endured, but for his children, his mood swings made for an almost crippling environment. On the one hand there was the angry, physically violent authority figure, and on the other there was a gentle, elegant loner, the "real" artist in the family, who was treated as a kind of mysterious genius whose beautiful fabrics and jewelry designs no one bought. It was my mother's art, her layouts for catalogues, that paid all the bills for their whole long lifetime together. That must have made Daddy feel inadequate, but he hid his disappointment by inventing himself as a genius whose passions included studying UFOs and teaching himself to read Egyptian hieroglyphics, Easter Island script, and cuneiform, as well as many modern languages. His library overflowed with books on every subject from art to astronomy, electricity to ancient history. He was a man whose gifts and intellectual curiosity would have been celebrated in another century, but unfortunately he lived out his days feeling like a failure. He was one of the most interesting men I have ever known. He looked a cross between Tyrone Power and Eugene O'Neill—the romantic genius with troubled eyes, capable of equal measures of unpredictable rage and tenderness at a moment's notice.

He met my mother when they were both struggling artists in New York during the Depression, and their marriage lasted until they died, two years apart, after forty-five years together. I never saw them fight or argue, but I never saw effusive affection either. They were people born at the turn of the century, my mother six years before him, and they both were extremely conservative, honorable, and disciplined. My brother and I were brought up with old-fashioned values, like honesty and a responsibility to contribute to the world in which we lived. One of my earliest memories is of my mother sorting out in neat stacks the monthly bills to be paid, and setting aside dollars for the specific charity requests that touched them. She taught me that I had an obligation to give something back to society, no matter how little that could be some months.

If my father was an exceptionally bright, complicated man, my mother was also remarkable. She had gone to college to be a scientist, but after graduation she went to Paris to study art, and that became her lifetime career. Unfortunately, she never gave herself credit for her talent, choosing instead to play the role of guardian of her husband's genius. She was strong, a real pioneer spirit. When she was in her early twenties she traveled all over the Middle East on her own, an unheard-of adventure at that time. There was nothing she could not do, and she had the ability to make the best of any situation. Over all of this was the innocence of a child, a quality of naïveté that made my mother unique.

When my brother and I were babies, my parents made the economic choice of moving into a two-family house in the country. Looking back on that choice, I think that it cost them their privacy and some of their dreams. The four of us were squashed into two bedrooms and a small living room; we shared the kitchen and one bathroom with our landlords, who were revolting elderly alcoholics.

Instead of enjoying the expansive, creative environment that I later invented for my *Time* cover, we lived in a home with almost no doors, no privacy, and an atmosphere of total asphyxiation. There were not a lot of light times in our house; it was all pretty serious.

We had no television, which in some ways was a blessing. Our entertainment consisted of drawing the flowers in the garden or the chickens in the backyard, or taking long walks in the nearby woods. My brother, although he was a year younger than I, was the more adventurous one—a brilliant and imaginative playmate. We collected autumn leaves and explored caves and made up elaborate fantasies hour after hour. Indoors, we read or played with our parents' art supplies. We learned to amuse ourselves in those childhood days, and I am forever grateful that my parents and circumstances taught me to be self-sufficient and curious, capable of being absorbed by even the smallest detail of a flower. When Daddy wanted to relax, he would go into the garden and sketch the flowers and the birds. He would hold a fuzzy dandelion between his fingers and say to me: "Look at this. Isn't it remarkable, perfect?" And I learned to see it, and everything else, acutely well. That was a big gift.

On certain special days I would accompany Daddy on the train to New York City for lunch at the Oyster Bar in Grand Central Station and an afternoon in the Egyptian wing of the Metropolitan Museum of Art. Other days we would go off to secondhand stores and junk shops, to the secret amusement of my mother, who thought we were both pack rats. It was part of the bond between Daddy and·me, just as my mother and I shared endless hours doing jigsaw puzzles or painting Easter eggs, enameling, or making cards for Christmas and Valentine's Day. These were wonderful hours for me, and even as a little girl I was aware of how unusual that time together was.

The unhealthy side of this life style was that we rarely saw anyone outside our own small family. No one came for dinner; we seldom went out. It was not exactly Norman Rockwell, and from early on I thought there was something really peculiar about our entire family: we didn't fit in. We were not "normal." My only friend was a neighbor who lived two miles away on the same dirt road. Ellin Messolonghites and I would meet, on our bikes or on foot, at the halfway point, a neighbor's cow pasture; there we would share our little-girl dreams, day after day. And although she moved far away and our lives took very different paths, we have remained close friends, connected somehow by those long-ago afternoons.

And so I invented my childhood for *Time*, coloring in the pages to make certain realities less lonely, decorating them with fantasy.

I grew up with nearly all the characteristics of both my father and my mother, the bad ones and the good ones. From Daddy I got my terrible mood swings and my "eye," and from Mummy her judgmentalism as well as her inner strength. In spite of all the darker moments I have learned to examine over these years, I am left with a great deal of gratitude and love for my parents. I have worked hard to understand their mistakes and choices, and I see clearly now that they were exceptional people surviving difficult circumstances with only the best in mind for their children.

Many years later I was blessed to be with each of them

at the actual moment of their deaths. I had been terrified of death for as long as I can remember, crying myself to sleep every night at the thought of one of them dying. Daddy's death came first, after years of crippling emphysema among other physical breakdowns.

I got the phone call just in time to make the last plane out of Los Angeles to New York, but I was not prepared for the sight of my poor father wired up in his hospital bed, frail and scared. I have always thought he deliberately got up that afternoon, against the nurse's orders, and in that short walk with his oxygen bottle to the bathroom, gave himself the fatal embolism that killed him several minutes later. As he went through the slow-motion contortions of death, I felt my own body leave the room and observe the experience from outside, simultaneously, while we held hands—my mother, my father, and me.

Two years later, just days before my forty-first birthday, when she was visiting Josh and me in Malibu, Mummy suffered a sudden heart attack. She "died" but recovered three times in the ambulance on the way to the hospital, so strong was her will to live.

That night, very late, I returned from the hospital where she had finally passed away. I was grateful to Bob for having been there with me for the whole ordeal, and grateful that Mummy's death had been quick; she was someone who could not have endured a long and terrible hospital stay. Exhausted and in a kind of sad shock, I came home to find Josh waiting up for me.

For several hours we stayed awake talking, while I explained to my nine-year-old that his grandmother's spirit had left her body to be with God. Finally, after all the questioning, he changed the subject to baseball, and I knew that he was satisfied with my answers. Just as he was dozing off to sleep, at about four in the morning, our big gray cat came to sleep on his bed. Josh said, "That cat never slept with me before, only with Grandma. I think that my grandma's spirit went into our cat." Perhaps so. She slept with one of us ever afterward.

As SAD and difficult as it was for me to be present at my parents' deaths, I know I was privileged to see and feel for myself that moment when the spirit fights free of the no-longer-healthy flesh. I could witness for myself that the now peaceful-looking receptacles of their souls had at last set them free to soar into eternity. And my nameless fear of death changed, so that today I am convinced that each of us must be permitted to decide for ourselves just when our own ill bodies are ready to release our spirits.

There has not been a day in the past decade that I have not been enriched by my parents' presence in my life. In that sense, they are immortal.

I n 1955, Hollywood released a film called *The Black-board Jungle*. It starred Glenn Ford as a high school teacher desperately trying to control and teach a roomful of anarchic teenagers, and it pretty much described the local high school where I might have gone. However, due to the interest of a wealthy and kind woman in town, I was offered a four-year scholarship at a private girls' school a half-hour's drive from home. Rosemary Hall—the Pink Prison, as we called it—opened my eyes and forever enlarged my dreams.

The school was founded at the beginning of the century by a distinguished feminist educator named Carolyn Ruutz-Rees, who believed that a strict education in the classics and Shakespeare, poetry, and languages would produce enlightened young women. She patterned the architecture of the school after buildings she had visited in Tuscany and planted the large grounds with beech trees and apple orchards, rich lawns for the two hockey fields, and numerous flowering shrubs. There was even the facsimile of an ancient Greek amphitheater, with a brook separating the "stage" from the audience. Each June the students would perform a different play by Shakespeare—featuring, of course, an all-girl cast. My only real acting experience prior to *Goodbye, Columbus* was as a series of men in these plays: from spearbearer in *Julius Caesar* to Lysander in *Midsummer Night's Dream,* to my final, starring chance as the king in *Henry IV, Part 1.* The high point of this performance came when I fell—fully clothed in chain mail knitted of twine, and clattering my tin sword—into the stony brook.

Rosemary Hall was full of rituals and traditions, which I loved. There were days set aside for winding daisies around a big tree, or for performing in the Nativity play in the chapel at Christmastime, or for reciting endless stanzas of poetry memorized over spring vacation. Annual prizes were awarded for excellence in every subject and the winners' names were illuminated in gold leaf on placards hung in the classrooms. Graduates' names were written in gold leaf on the ceiling of the chapel, and art students were invited to keep the records of the chapel in an elaborately decorated parchment book. We had to wear uniforms, and so we all, rich and poor alike, looked the same. Our velvet hats were passed from friend to friend, generation to generation—another tradition.

The school was equally divided between the girls who commuted each day, like me, and those who boarded. Many of these boarders were wealthy little girls from broken or unhappy homes, and it was easy to understand why a number of them were thrilled to get an invitation for the weekend. I look back with a certain shame at the secret embarrassment I felt when several of these girls stayed at our house. I was upset that we lived in a two-family house, and that my mother preferred not to wear a wedding ring, that we did not own a television set, that we didn't have money, that my clothes were so "sensible," and on and on. I completely missed the point that I had a generous and interesting family whom my friends adored. I was too caught up in my own materialism and desire to appear "normal," whatever that meant.

I excelled in academics, and I was elected to one student government position after another. I appeared to be the Model Student, and for my four years at Rosemary Hall I devoted myself to being Perfect. In doing so I received an invaluable education, one that enabled me to obtain the scholarship I needed to go on to college. But my obsessive need to do everything right cost me a lot of fun and spontaneity. I never saw a boy, had a date, did any of the usual teenage things. I chose my friends one at a time, and while I was probably respected by my peers for the good work I was constantly doing, I don't think I was ever popular, in that scary teenage sense. I was too zealous about my job of giving out demerits for bad behavior, too righteous when I saw other girls cheating in exams. Now I can look back to my behavior then and see beneath the surface of that schoolgirl to the woman who would become judgmental and tight.

Toward the end of my days at Rosemary Hall I was asked to a dance at another school. Terrified because I had never been to a boys' school, much less danced, I worked up the courage to go. On the dreaded day I stood in the kitchen, ironing a borrowed outfit—probably a status poodle skirt—and began to cry. I just could not go, I told my mother. She said, very firmly, "Listen, you have to assume that every single person in that room is as insecure as you are. You can't wait for them to come to you. You have to make the first effort."

In years to come I learned that most of us are indeed nervous socially. We are afraid we have nothing to say, that we are not witty, that we have on the wrong costume—our own skins. And I learned to drink, very specifically because it made all those uncomfortable feelings go away.

One other thing my mother said to me comes to mind: "Whatever you decide to do in life, be sure that the joy of doing it does not depend upon the applause of others, because in the long run we are, all of us, alone."

To a child, the word *alone* sounds frighteningly like *lonely;* but I have come to know that my mother meant that we must all be able to entertain ourselves, feel whole and fulfilled without the approval of others. How ironic that I ultimately chose to be in a business in which you do not even exist without this approval.

At Rosemary Hall, I received a difficult and inspiring liberal arts education, which would open all kinds of doors for me for the rest of my life. I learned to have respect for tradition and history, for ritual and celebration. Sitting there in that romantically Victorian, Tuscan-pink building, I fantasized about the lives of independent, exciting women in times gone by. I had big, romantic dreams, and Rosemary Hall taught me that if I worked hard and honorably, there was no reason why a lot of them couldn't come true.

In the summer of 1958, I took a job waiting on tables at Haddon Hall, the only WASP hotel on the boardwalk in Atlantic City, for what turned out to be my first typical teenage summer. We worked very hard, but for the first time in my life I had Gidget-like evenings of beer and necking, a social life, and even a real boyfriend. I shared a small monastic room with the wildest girl I had ever met—a redheaded Roman Catholic who masqueraded as Miss Quiet during work hours, and spent nights having major sex with a very hot-looking Puerto Rican dishwasher. I envied her uninhibited life. But I stayed up, night after night, and although I wasn't having sex yet, I joined the other kids on the beach for beer parties and rock and roll, and felt part of a teenage group at last. I remember I was very thin that summer, subsisting on shrimp and vanilla ice cream stolen from the

Cockatoo Lounge, where I worked the breakfast and lunch shifts.

There was an odd innocence about our part of Atlantic City then. I had taken the bus from New York City and passed ghost towns of Jersey Shore summer spots— places where people had gone earlier in the century to play in the lazy summer surf and pose for timeless watercolors by Winslow Homer. One of those towns was completely overrun by wild roses and wisteria, like a mysterious secret garden from the thirties. Even Atlantic City—and Haddon Hall in particular—had a certain sweetness, light-years removed from the decayed honky-tonk of its current incarnation as Las Vegas East.

IN AUGUST of every year, the Miss America Pageant came to Atlantic City, and most hotels hosted a meal for the contestants; the Pageant was part of the lifeblood of the city's tourist trade. We in the lunch room of Haddon Hall served a late breakfast to the fifty beauties, and it was an experience not to be missed. Each contestant came with her duenna, an older woman whose job was to keep the beauty's virginal demeanor intact during Pageant week, as well as to remind her to cross her ankles and wipe the corners of her lipsticked mouth like a lady.

Every hotel had a float in the parade, and ours was constructed with a gigantic heart in the center. The float was covered with roses and had a long rope swing in the middle, from which would swing and wave a hotel waitress: me. At each corner stood another waitress. We were quite a sight in our little bathing suits and ballet slippers and tacky makeup. There we were, hour after hour after hour, waving at the crowd, which stretched for miles along the boardwalk. Later a photographer took a borderline pinup shot of me in my Cockatoo Lounge sleeveless Dacron blouse, and parrot-striped dirndl skirt, with a wide banner proclaiming MISS HADDON HALL across my chest. My parents must have choked when the picture ran in our local newspaper.

After the endless day was over, the owner of the hotel, a nice man from Philadelphia, Mr. Lippincott, took his five starring waitresses to dinner. I remember that we ate our first and only steaks of the summer, which we fell upon ravenously and gratefully after all the vanilla ice cream, beer, and stolen shrimp.

Probably because my own mother was not married until she was almost forty, I never thought about marriage while I was going to high school or even during much of college. Marriage wasn't something to think or dream about until you had first had a chance to "do everything." I had some vague romantic notion that I was, like my mother, an unusually independent woman with things to do—not that I had any idea what they were. I hoped they included exotic voyages along the lines of Lady Jane Digby's, or some important contribution to art, like Georgia O'Keeffe or Isadora Duncan.

Then along came "Alex."

He was a year ahead of me in college, the quintessential Harvard man who had been to school in Europe and spoke four or five languages interchangeably. He was sophisticated, smart, and traffic-stoppingly handsome. We began to see each other on weekends. He was definitely the Big Catch, and I was pretty insecure until it became apparent that we were in love. After he had graduated from Harvard, he had joined the ROTC and gone away somewhere. We wrote long, loving letters to each other, and my senior year at Wellesley College was an agony of missing him. Apart from the hours I spent painting in the art studio, all I thought about that year was Alex. When he came back, we decided to marry.

I imagine he was as surprised as I was to find himself engaged. I wore the beautiful topaz and diamond ring he gave me and tried to figure out how to be a traditional bride, trousseau and all, on the $54 a week I was earning at my first job as an editorial assistant at *Harper's Bazaar*. Alex began a very demanding job in the international division of a major bank. Real life had begun, and it was nothing at all like the wildly romantic weekends we had shared at Harvard and at his parents' place in the Adirondacks. The terrible truth about my relationship with Alex was that it was a perfect romance, but I was unprepared for the tough realities of two young people starting out their lives together on their own.

His father was a famous and adored surgeon, and his mother a gentle beauty whom everyone worshiped. The family were very close, which I loved, and they were very social, which terrified me. In spite of my equally good education and very "fine" upbringing, I felt inadequate to these nice people for whom country clubs and the cocktail circuit and trips to Europe were everyday reality.

So I learned to drink. I knew nothing about such social amenities as when it was all right to drink a Bloody Mary with breakfast, or just how to stir the perfect martini.

Like joint-rolling ten years later, the ritual bored me, but my ignorance made me feel gauche. So, hoping that I looked as ravishingly blasé and rich as the coolly elegant flapper in a Fitzgerald story, I picked up my gin and tonic and posed in ways that made me feel mysterious and attractive. I also drank the gin and tonics, lots of them, and the first weekend I spent at Alex's house I threw up in the hedge and was carried up to my room. His parents were wonderfully understanding at breakfast the next morning, having had a lot of practice with inebriated guests in a society in which big-time drinking was part of the code.

But from the instant I took my first drink, I loved it; I felt pretty and witty and bright. Not phony and uncomfortable. And I gave myself permission to be something I never dared to be sober: uninhibited, even promiscuous, and out of control.

I knew how lucky I was to have been chosen by Alex, whom every woman was after. He came up to my parents' house to ask them formally for my hand in marriage. I stayed wide-awake in my nun-size cot in my childhood bedroom as he summoned the gallantry to ask Daddy if he would let his naïve and virginal daughter marry him. I shall never forget Daddy's reply: calmly he suggested that perhaps we should wait awhile, let college days slip away and real life begin. When the subject was brought up again the next day, I loftily suggested to my romantic father that he did "not know anything about love." In spite of Daddy's sage advice, we went ahead.

I am now pretty sure that while my parents knew I was lucky to have Alex, they also realized he would be even luckier to escape me. While my mother gave me the impression that she was a little worried that I might be drinking too much on college weekends, I always got the feeling that Daddy secretly enjoyed this side of me, which he and I shared. Although he had kept his promise to my mother, not ever taking a drink when my brother and I were growing up, he somehow convinced her—and himself—that "a little beer" would be all right now that so many years had gone by. From the moment he picked up that first beer, my last year in college, he drank alcoholically again. It was a classic case—not that any of us was educated enough to spot it. I think he liked the fact that one other person in the house was also breaking away from my mother's watchful and disciplined ways. It might even have been an unspoken—perhaps unconscious—bond between us. We wallowed in our notions of ourselves as moody "artists" capable of huge romantic gestures, never mind the wake we left.

When Daddy hesitated to sanction my first marriage, I am sure he was thinking of Alex. (That goes for the next two husbands as well, I am afraid.) Somewhere there is a club, one of those wonderful high-ceilinged mahogany places where men gather in the pink twilight to breathe deeply together in manly camaraderie before going home to face their women. There is a small group of these men, cozy in their squeaky old leather chairs by the fire, raising their collective glasses on high to celebrate their great good fortune in having escaped being married to me.

For over a year Alex and I lived in an apartment the size of one of his parents' closets. The two of us could not stand sideways in the kitchen at the same time. If we forgot to buy milk for the coffee, it was a four-flight walk to the street below. My parents generously offered to paint over the ghastly green interior, but it took only six weeks for their two coats of white paint to turn brilliant yellow.

No more parties, no more wild times. Just two young people going to their nine-to-five jobs and wondering where all the excitement had gone.

REAL LIFE.

I was not good at it, and I poisoned a potentially decent relationship with my disappointment.

When we ended it, I blocked out all feelings except for the ones I had about freedom. I picked the Fourth of July to go to Tijuana for my divorce. Today I feel remorse for the selfish, hurtful way in which I behaved— but Alex was certainly well out of it. I hope he has lived happily ever after. He deserves to.

August 22, 1989. Diana Vreeland died today, and I am very saddened by the news. In 1960, when I graduated from Wellesley and briefly dreamed of being a powerhouse in the fashion business, I landed the great magazine job of all time: as Mrs. Vreeland's assistant at *Harper's Bazaar*.

"Assistant" was different from "secretary." The latter was a tough, smart woman who typed, and with whom I shared Mrs. Vreeland's outer office. Pat and I arrived punctually at nine o'clock to begin our half-hour phone meeting with "DV," who was still, I imagined, up to her neck in hot, scented bubble bath. That phone call was a monologue of fierce orders in anticipation of her arrival at the office later in the morning. I would already have been to her apartment at 550 Park Avenue, because my pre-office assignment was to carry her portfolio the eight blocks to work. (Pat normally took it home at the end of the day. DV was never seen carrying anything as mundane as an attaché case.) As I waited timidly in the hallway of the brilliant-red paisleyed apartment, I could smell Irish oatmeal cooking, as well as a scent new to me: last night's Rigaud candles. Her husband, T. Reed Vreeland, was the first to import these now-familiar candles, and back then the very existence of a scented—as opposed to a utilitarian—candle was to me exotic and rich. On his way out of the apartment to work, Mr. Vreeland, beautifully dressed in the style of the Duke of Windsor, would say hello in his quiet manner; and that was all the contact I would get from anyone, except for the maid's goodbye as she handed me the fat portfolio.

I was awed by what I saw in that apartment: silver-framed Avedon photographs of everyone I had ever heard of, row upon row of antique silver boxes from England, and Scottish horn snuffboxes fastidiously lined up on table surfaces. There were shelves upon shelves of wonderful books and Persian miniatures, and everywhere, Billy Baldwin's scarlet paisley. I had never seen anything like the way she lived—the luxury and theatrics of this very personal apartment.

I don't know what I thought I was getting into, working at *Harper's Bazaar*, and for Mrs. Vreeland in particular: camel hair coats and nice little color coordinates? It was the height of the glamorous and daring fashion magazine era, and nothing and no one was too outrageous to be photographed and lionized. A very rich woman, preferably with a European husband of dubious royal lineage, became an international beauty overnight with the single stroke of Mrs. Vreeland's approving pen. At the same time, Mrs. Vreeland had such an eye that she was able to spot specialness in some very ordinary girls, who, with her blessing and Avedon's lens, became the superstar models of the Sixties. As I crawled around the floor of Mrs. Vreeland's office, arranging row upon row of shoes and belts and paste necklaces in preparation for the monthly run-through of all the clothing submitted for the upcoming issue of the magazine, I envied the stardom of some of these women.

To Diana Vreeland, I was "Girl!" "Girl, bring me a pencil." "Girl, get me Babe Paley on the phone." "Girl, confirm lunch with Isak Dinesen at La Côte Basque." One day, as I struggled on the carpet to arrange violet snakeskin shoes for a photo shoot, Mrs. Vreeland swept dramatically by me, throwing her heavy Mainbocher overcoat at me, and I involuntarily chucked it right back at her. "That is the rudest Girl I have ever known!"

Oh, she was tough. But in the six months I worked for her at $54 a week, I learned more about style and color and fashion than I ever learned before, or since. As long as I could get her off the tyrannical subject of magazine work, I was enthralled. Sometimes I could get her to talk about Diaghilev's Ballets Russes (she of course had seen them), or Goya, or her favorite topic: India. Sometimes I accompanied her on the short walk home (to carry the portfolio, of course), and was educated every time. I had never heard of or smelled freesias: "Cecil Beaton brought these to me at lunch." I knew nothing about the Windsors and had never been to Paris—or anywhere. I learned to "see" by listening to her. Whether or not her colorful life story was real or partly fantasy made no difference. I was mesmerized by the possibilities of her life, by the people she knew and the style she invented. She was a star and an original in a business that has never had very many of either, and I was lucky to be around her even for that short while. She gave me a taste of what might be.

It was interesting that while she advocated the most outrageous clothing, hair, and makeup in the pages of her magazine, she—unlike the editor groupies—never really fell into the trap of "What am I supposed to wear this week?" (Translation: unless I want to be OUT.) Day after day she looked exactly the same: little black sweater and black Mainbocher skirt, funny little handmade black T-strap pumps, hair so black that it was nearly navy-blue, and a gold wedding ring on a hand whose nails were perfectly manicured a brilliant scarlet, matching her huge mouth. Her walk was a kind of pelvic-thrust caricature of a model's runway walk. And her words were pronouncements: hilarious, outrageous, dead-on.

Once a mousy, nice little man came to the office with a huge and clumsy armload of pen-line drawings of shoes: Andy Warhol before Pop Art. And I remember the office door closing with heavy drama every time a certain breathy voice came on the phone: Jacqueline Kennedy conferring with DV on her "look" for the White House reign. And I remember rock stars and sexy young girls who came to the office to pay homage to someone whose approval opened doors throughout the Who's Who world of pop and fashion power. She was a star-maker in the great Hollywood tradition, and that energy is what kept her ageless and vitally interesting.

When I was offered a job for twice as much money as the Hearst organization was paying me, she said, "My dear Girl, you can't leave; you don't know enough." I knew she was right, but I needed the money.

Years after I had left *Bazaar* and become a movie star, she seemed to be a bit more interested in me, particularly as I was married to a handsome, powerful, rich man. She even stayed interested through my tabloid-soaked marriage to the Biggest Movie Star in the World. But after that, I never heard from her, and it made me sad, because she was someone whose approval I would like to have earned, with or without my famous husbands. But perhaps I seemed to lack focus, to play everything too safe at that time, for her to find me exciting enough to be singled out and collected.

She pushed everything to the limit and had fun, even while she scared some of us to death. I miss the knowledge that she is here somewhere, conjuring up brilliant, impossible visions. God rest her soul.

W hile there were large chunks of *Goodbye, Columbus, Love Story, Just Tell Me What You Want,* even *The Winds of War* that were challenging and fun, in many ways the best job of my life was working as a photo stylist for the fashion photographer Melvin Sokolsky.

I first met Melvin when I was trying to get work as a college model, and I had followed his work ever since. His and Richard Avedon's were the photographs I admired the most, and each month when I got my advance copy of the magazine and read it on the train trip home, I always looked for his pictures. They had extraordinary lighting, a very original point of view, and a quality of timelessness.

I first met Melvin when he appeared one day in Diana Vreeland's office—a slight, intense blond man clutching a portfolio of black-and-white photographs—an assignment for the next issue. I was excited to meet him, and surprised to discover he was a quiet, rather shy man. However, that was only part of him. The other Melvin, I soon came to know, was a wild man: egotistical, challenging, outspoken, and really smart. I liked him immediately.

At that time I was engaged to be married to Alex, and my future in-laws wanted my photograph in the social section of *The New York Times*. I could not afford to pay a society photographer for the typical starry-eyed wedding portrait, and Diana Vreeland's secretary suggested I ask Melvin Sokolsky to take the picture. She told me he was very sweet and would probably be glad to help me out.

I was thrilled when he agreed, and we arranged to meet in his tiny studio, which was the ground floor of a little red brick building where he lived with his family. I have never forgotten the image that greeted me there. In the living room, taking up most of the space and surrounded by no-seam paper, was a ping-pong table with beautiful glasses and Granny Smith apples arranged on it. It looked more like an eighteenth-century Dutch still life than the setup for a beer advertisement.

Someone at the magazine had managed to get me into a wholesale house for a wedding dress, and I arrived carrying a simple white gown that I hoped would look like a Balenciaga. It had a short cape to cover the bare top, and with the cape turned around, I looked like a Velázquez portrait. (At least I hoped I did.) We fussed a bit with the veil, and did the picture. It was hardly the typical wedding portrait, but I thought it was beautiful.

My mother-in-law was not so crazy about it: she told me I looked too "hard."

When we finished the wedding photograph, Melvin said, "You have great taste. Why don't you come work for me? I'll pay you ninety-five dollars a week." I hesitated for half a second, because I knew that working for Diana Vreeland was an extraordinary opportunity in the fashion business. But this was almost twice as much money, and besides, I already had a terrific feeling about the studio and about Melvin. He was at an exciting point in his career, as was the whole industry. It was the early Sixties, a feast time for fashion and fantasy. Because of Diana Vreeland, every assignment from *Harper's Bazaar* was a guarantee that we could go mad with our imaginations. Not only was the fashion itself often exciting, but there was the added satisfaction of knowing that the pictures would be flawlessly laid out by Henry Wolf, one of the most important art directors of the era.

My job was . . . everything. The only thing I had nothing to do with was the cameras themselves. (I still don't know how to use a light meter.)

One part of my job was to book the models; another was to show Melvin the portfolios of new models I thought he would like. I also had to stock the dressing room and have accessories on hand for clients who didn't have the budget to justify my running all over town for special jewelry and props. I was also responsible for arranging treats for the more spoiled models, who swept into the studio as theatrically as Gloria Swanson: "Mel, could you have the girl [that was me] get me an extra-thick raspberry ice cream soda, and put on Diana Ross singing 'Baby Love'?" Some girls who walked into that

studio were so breathtakingly beautiful that they stopped
traffic; others needed every bit of assistance possible from
the hairdresser, the makeup man, and even me with my
bicycle tape and safety pins. There is a well-known TV
actress who began as a particularly nice, and funny,
model; she had a great face, but no breasts. One day my
job was to wrap her skinny little torso in strategically
placed duct tape, creating the cleavage necessary to make
Helen Gurley Brown happy for her *Cosmopolitan* cover.

I could do it.

I could also iron gigantic taffeta ball gowns and crin-
olines on the toilet seat of a motor home if we were
shooting out in the middle of nowhere. If an impatient
client was waiting, counting the money his model was
costing, I could get to Bloomingdale's and back faster
than anyone I knew when we needed a certain wineglass
for a still life. I knew where on 39th Street to get double-
faced satin ribbon and real silk flowers, which came packed
from Paris in lovely lettuce-green dress boxes. I knew
where to rent a boa constrictor; I knew which stores
would lend things for credit and which ones would rent
them; and I knew which dealers of fine antique furniture
would take the time to tell me just why one chair was
more valuable than another, or which artist really did the
work on a certain silver bowl. Special places like the
(then) Ginsburg & Levy gallery for fine American art, or
James Robinson for English silver, come to mind. Or that
unique and wonderful series of rooms on First Avenue,
the Newel Art Galleries. These assignments taught me
more than I ever imagined, and they gave me tools I have
used ever since. My education in fine things, as well as

in hard-to-get ones, took place during those six years with Sokolsky.

One of the most interesting places where I found assistance was the American Museum of Natural History. I love that museum, and the curatorial staff and display artists were always extremely generous with their help. Once, when it was altogether the wrong time of year, we had to do a whiskey ad against a background of autumn leaves at their peak. The artists of the museum did a huge background painting for us. It was so well executed that in the finished ad it was impossible to tell that the model had not been photographed in the Adirondacks, sipping her drink on a crisp October day. And once the museum lent us feathers and shells when I had to convert the face of a craggy old black man, whom we recruited from a street corner, into a Mud Man from New Guinea for a portrait of: a man smoking a cigarette.

There was almost always something insane going on at the studio. We worked around the clock, and it was usually great fun, except when Melvin slept late. Then we all had to cover for him, and when he arrived at the last minute, unprepared to deal with some high-paying advertising client, he would blame us for whatever was missing. As much as I loved him, I wanted to strangle him then. Those times were outweighed, however, by the affection I felt for him and for his wife, Button, and his younger brother, Stanley. For six years they were like family to me, and the relationship we enjoyed in the name of "work" was one of the happiest, most supportive ones of my whole life.

Melvin was endlessly curious, and I was forever haunting old bookstores to add to his growing library of great reference books. I bought art books of every imaginable sort, rare, out-of-print volumes that provided rich inspiration for many, many photographs, as well as an education for me.

I suppose my favorite assignment while I worked at the Sokolsky studio had to be going to Paris with Melvin to photograph the spring collections for *Harper's Bazaar*. This was a very big deal for Melvin, and his first time to do it. He had come up with the idea of photographing the models suspended over Paris (it was freezing January) in a huge transparent ball, which would seem to float over all the familiar monuments. For page after page. He had an enormous plastic ball fabricated in two halves, then crated and shipped to Paris. And he devised a way to hang it from a crane. Melvin did not speak a word of French, and as I had at least studied the language in high school for four years, my job was to interpret, as well as to locate a crane and make the other arrangements for the dozens of locations we would need.

I had never been to Europe, and it was all terribly exciting to me. I will never forget that first sight of Paris as we drove through one of those magnificent gates just as the sun came up. I was high with the thrill of the city for every second of every sleepless day and night of our ten-day trip.

The fashion business takes itself unbelievably seriously, and the collections, which are presented twice a year, have all the mystery and self-important drama of a major theatrical opening. The spring collection is all about "Which clothes are we going to make you wear next fall?" The answer is: "Nothing you already have in your closet." So an expensively organized publicity hype promotes the collection, in much the same way as the studios cover the media with lavish publicity for a new film. Part of this elaborate performance is that the new styles are all closely guarded, to build the anticipation before that first runway show. Editors and their photographers fight over which one of them gets to photograph a favored dress first. It is not unusual to have a special costume rushed by taxi at three o'clock in the morning to one photographer, before making the rounds twenty minutes later to another studio, and another fashion editor, for another magazine.

For Melvin's first collection, we arrived with our so-called crystal ball. There were only a few days in which to organize the hideously complicated arrangements necessary for shooting all over Paris. I spent hours and hours with the Paris police, who were amazingly helpful and more than a little amused by the traffic complications we were causing.

For one photograph we decided to float the sphere in the middle of a narrow street in an ancient suburb of Paris. The crane could hardly fit. The dress of the moment arrived by taxi in the cold predawn, and by the time the model was dressed and had entered the sphere and been hoisted up, the pale winter sun had just come up. I shall never forget the sight of the little schoolchildren in their navy-blue uniforms, gaping in amazement at the big crystal ball floating over their heads as they marched off to class.

For another picture Melvin asked me to find a circus fire-eater to blow flames close to the ball as it drifted along over the Seine, much to the apprehension of the Dior-clad model inside.

Because I was translating for Melvin, I had the opportunity of spending an afternoon with Coco Chanel. It can be argued that in the history of twentieth-century fashion there has been no one more influential or revolutionary than Chanel, and the opportunity to meet her was a privilege. She had the reputation of being very difficult and very demanding of the photographers who were sent to record her collections. Because she had not met Melvin (and had recently quarreled with another *Bazaar* photographer), she summoned him to her famous apartment and atelier at 29–31, rue Cambon. We spent an hour in that often-photographed room while she scrutinized Melvin against a background of black lacquer and gold leaf, like a stage set. She evidently approved of him, and we were taken into her salon to watch the final editing of her collection. Chanel was herself dressed in her famous uniform—black suit with braid and gold buttons, little white shirt showing at the throat and wrists, and pounds of gold chains and costume jewelry. The look is as perfect today as it was then, and as it was decades before, when she invented it. On her head was her signature hat, and around her neck, in addition to the jewelry, pearls, and Maltese crosses, were her dressmaking scissors, hanging from a black grosgrain ribbon. She was a tiny woman, with fiery black eyes and the darting energy of a nervous blackbird.

As each model came out from behind a curtain, she was accompanied by a specific tailor assigned to the suit or dress she was wearing. These poor souls looked to me like bakers, dressed in cream-colored cotton work coats and nearly trembling in anticipation of the judgment ahead. One by one these pairs paraded before Chanel, and one by one they returned backstage, the costume in ribbons, literally cut in pieces by those lethal scissors. What looked to me each time like a flawlessly cut and fitted garment was unacceptable to Chanel. She orchestrated this performance for celebrities and wealthy customers as a kind of sneak preview. It was high theater, and Chanel enjoyed it immensely. It was a privilege to see the working of one of the very last of a breed of *hautes couturiers*—a woman whose taste and unfailing sense of the modern made her, like Diana Vreeland, a true genius in her field.

I ALWAYS enjoyed location work. I remember one assignment for a Volkswagen catalogue; we were to photograph "the Bug" all across the California countryside, from Palm Springs to Bakersfield. It was wonderful to be in the brilliant sunshine of Southern California that first time. It was every corny postcard and movie still I had ever seen: palm trees and fifties architecture and freeways as far as the eye could see. I felt I had landed on another planet. One day we rounded a corner to find a huge hill that was blue on one side and gold on the other. I thought the effect was caused by the sun and its shadows until we got closer and saw that one side was ablaze with yellow-orange California poppies and the other with violet lupine. It was the best of California, giving no hint of the overdevelopment and smog to come.

As we stopped to photograph the car against various backgrounds, we would rely on local talent for the models. One of these was a cowboy right out of Central Casting: a squinty-eyed, sunburned man with the lean body of the Marlboro Man. I love cowboys, and my heart stopped a little. Melvin noticed it and said with a smile, "You better hope he doesn't take off his hat; your illusions will be shattered." And so they were, some moments later: he was totally bald.

Melvin asked the impossible of all of us, and amazingly, we learned to deliver it: that was part of the work and part of the fun. The most outrageous project we ever undertook required that I stage a train wreck and various other disasters for a mega-montage being produced for an insurance-company advertisement. The single picture had to include a burning building, an elevator crash, a bunch of petty thieves doing their thing, and other outrageous mishaps that would be covered by a good insurance policy. We set this madness up in a run-down part of New Jersey, at a railroad yard where, for the *pièce de résistance,* I managed to persuade a rather stunned official to derail a train for us. It was great fun, a kids' game for grownups.

I spent six years working at the Sokolsky Studio, and by the time I left, there was almost nothing in the way of a prop or a background that I didn't know how to locate. I was a walking Yellow Pages, and the adventure soon became not "Can I find it?" but "How exactly do I find it?" I knew New York City from one end to another.

When I look back on those times, I know there was a kind of innocence that is hard for me to grasp today. We were taking pictures and creating ads when rock stars did not get $10 million just to hold the can of Pepsi. No model made a million dollars by endorsing a lipstick. It seems to me that the visual end of advertising, and even of editorial work, was more inventive and exciting then.

I don't know if those campaigns brought in comparable revenue, but I do know that everybody—ad executives, art directors, and photographers together—had to come up with images to stop the reader dead in his tracks. It was a constant education, and I had that job at the very best time.

After those six years I felt I had learned about as much as I ever would about styling photographs, and I thought it was time to try something new. It was a difficult decision, because of the deep friendships that had developed, and I didn't really know what it was I wanted to do next. I wondered about trying to run an art gallery, but realized that I probably did not know enough about any one phase of art to qualify. Although I did occasional modeling assignments, I knew that I was too uncomfortable—and irregular-looking—to make that a career. I continued to do some free-lance work for Melvin, helping him organize a series of photographs of the new British model Twiggy posing with all kinds of other famous people, from Wilt Chamberlain to Muhammad Ali. That was fun, but the assignment did not give me the same rush as it had when I was working with Sokolsky exclusively. It was time to move on.

In the last half-dozen years I have been able to put to good use the remarkable visual education I received as Melvin's stylist. I have designed house interiors for a number of friends, and the work has been stimulating and refreshingly devoid of the fearfulness that seems to haunt me in a lot of my film work. I guess that I feel rather secure about my so-called "eye," and while each job has been challenging, they all have been fun.

Certainly none of them was ever more rewarding than

the sprawling twenty-five-room clapboard "cottage" that I renovated for John Calley, the bright, generous, funny Warner Brothers executive. Besides the sheer joy of doing a wonderful old house on a tiny island off Connecticut, I had the rare experience of working for a friend who had so much confidence in me and in my ability that he gave me carte blanche with every detail.

It has taken me a while to realize that what I have been doing for fun all these years is something I can do well enough to have a second career. Several times I have treated the work too casually, believing that a contract was not necessary to ensure I would be treated like a professional. In spite of those sobering lessons, I look forward to doing more design work. The research and the work itself are challenging and soothing, and I am able to do it with no fear whatsoever of other people's "reviews." It is a kind of closure to the circle that began with Melvin Sokolsky and his family.

My years in the fashion business and with Sokolsky took me through most of what we have all come to think of as one of the great decades of this century, the sixties. In many ways, I was a creature of the sixties, although I was too frightened of drugs to try them. One of my dormitory mates at college had volunteered to take acid under Timothy Leary's surveillance at Harvard one summer, and most of my friends smoked pot. But scared as I was of losing control, I preferred to drink lots and lots of wine, oblivious to the fact that I was getting high my own way.

I dressed the part of the Flower Child—miniskirts and beads and antique thrift-shop clothes—and I gave the closest approximation I dared of a Free Spirit. I marched in the great peace marches, protesting the Vietnam War and segregation, and feeling convinced, as we all did, that our generation could change the world.

I became romantically involved with several men in succession, and lived with each of them for several years, thinking all the while how terribly "modern" I was. And, inevitably, I got pregnant, at a time when neither I nor my very loving and supportive boyfriend felt it was the right time for us to have children. Then, in pre–Roe versus Wade times, we had to face the alternative of an illegal abortion. After a harrowing period of trying to decide if we were making the right moral decision, we decided to go ahead with the operation.

By the time we located a man who would perform the abortion for a price we could afford, several months had gone by and I had reached the point in my pregnancy where I had to deal with it immediately, for safety's sake. I was desperate and frightened, and the sight of this doctor's location did nothing to allay my fears.

I remember a seedy hotel on New York's Upper West Side, with a constant stream of wretched people walking in and out. I assumed that their business was drugs or prostitution. I was no less uncomfortable when I got off the elevator on the eighteenth floor and entered a shabby waiting room. I was dressed in immaculate summer cottons, and even now I can feel my body sitting straight and proper, like a schoolgirl's, as I waited for my "turn." And I waited all day—eight hours to be exact. My boyfriend had parked on the street below, and every half hour I would go to the window to reassure myself that he was still there, that I was not alone and unprotected up there in that strange office. I did not understand why I was being kept waiting, why I had been told to be there at nine o'clock precisely, and yet had seen single women and even couples come and go all day long, ahead of me. I wanted to cry, I wanted to scream, I wanted to run away, but I couldn't; I was out of time, and I knew it.

Finally, as it was getting dark, there were only two patients left—myself and another girl. I asked her if she would mind waiting for me when she was through, as I was evidently going to be the last one admitted and I didn't want to be there alone. The doctor—to whom I had not been introduced all day—overheard her saying she would wait for me, and he became furious. He ordered her to leave and demanded to know how I had dared to speak to one of his clients. With that, he locked the door, and it was then that I became really frightened, even hysterical. I assumed he was going to rape me, maybe kill me, and there I was, all alone on the eighteenth floor of a decrepit old building. He ordered me to be quiet, because by now he was fearful that my cries were going to arouse suspicions in the building.

And then he changed. He calmly told me to get hold of myself, and asked if my boyfriend was still around. I could see his car parked below. The doctor told me to bring him up to the office, where I would receive an injection that would produce severe cramps and a miscarriage. I was to return at seven the next morning for a necessary D and C.

I realized then that the doctor was as afraid of the situation as I was: if he made a mistake, or was caught performing the illegal procedure, he faced certain jail and the end of his practice. As he was obviously a foreigner,

I assumed that he could be thrown out of the country as well. In a way, his life was also on the line.

Getting the injection was simple and quick enough, but I shall never forget my first glimpse of that inner office: perhaps my memory and imagination distort it, but I remember a small, none-too-clean room with a steel table and a steel tray containing sharp little steel instruments. In spite of his white jacket, there was nothing about this doctor's scared and weary demeanor to inspire confidence.

After my shot, we drove home. I was so exhausted that I could barely get up the next morning for the seven o'clock appointment. The doctor was less abrupt when I saw him then, and I have a faint memory of the sound and even of the lightest touch of the instrument as it scraped inside of me—nothing more. I was high on sodium pentathol.

Abortion is a very serious act, but I have always believed strongly in freedom of choice. There is enough anguish involved in making the very private decision of whether to have an abortion without having to deal with government intervention. If this country again makes abortion illegal, poor women are the ones who are going to get hurt. Rich women, in my experience, can always pay enough money to have a safe "illegal" abortion. If you do not have that kind of money, an already anguishing experience is further complicated by real fears about unsafe, unsanitary, even life-threatening conditions.

The decision to have an abortion is such a complicated, personal one that there should be no place whatsoever for government intrusion. I think that all the government should do is damn well make sure that the clinics are safe.

When I am asked if I think that abortion is about killing a living thing, I cannot answer that question, except for myself. Abortion is not a kind of birth control; it is not a convenience. It is one of the most heart-wrenching, difficult decisions of a woman's life. Sometimes she has the loving support of the man involved, and sometimes she does not. Sometimes she can turn to friends and family and even church for support, and sometimes she cannot. But in the end it is not only her body that is involved, but other issues, much more difficult to define. There is her personal sense of right and wrong. And there is the whole question of precisely when it is that the soul enters into life as we know it. These cannot be legislated.

I have spent an enormous amount of time in the past four years working with unwanted, battered kids, whose own home lives were so desperate that they had turned to drugs to soften the pain of their reality. And I do not know which is worse: abortion, or an unwanted child. The latter may be in for a life sentence of lovelessness and horror, and that is an important fact to consider. There is a facile answer to this, but where are the thousands and thousands of adoptive parents needed to love and care for those children whose age or pedigree make them somehow "undesirable"?

When a woman decides to have a child, that is the single most important decision of her life. I think everything else goes around it. Everything.

And if she is not prepared to make that the central event in her life, then I think what she is going to do to that little soul is more horrifying than dealing with it in early pregnancy.

This is a story of Ali, her Ego, and Salvador Dali. I didn't get the joke at the time, but today it makes me laugh.

It began one evening in 1963 when I was invited to a cocktail party for a bizarre collection of people, which included Richard Nixon and Salvador Dali (whose art I had disliked intensely for as long as I could remember). Suddenly there was Dali himself in front of me, leaning on his cloisonné-topped walking stick and muttering something about wanting to do a painting of me, while his wife, Gala, eyed us from across the room with a kind of predatory glitter. At once, my ego conjured up the scenario: a gigantic portrait of Ali MacGraw by Salvador Dali—never mind that I hated his work—to be hung, sooner or later, where the Winged Victory of Samothrace stands in the Louvre.

Of course I would pose for him! A chance for immortality. So, later that week, I left work early and crosstown-bused my way to the King Cole Bar in the St. Regis Hotel, where Dali held court for the likes of me every afternoon. What a motley crew we were, sitting silent while Dali checked us out in his secret, eccentric way. As I finished my drink he suggested to me that I should come back the next day to be sketched. And so, dressed in my aquamarine fake Chanel suit, I arrived once more at the King Cole Bar and was ushered up to a most peculiar room he leased in the hotel. There was an atrocious collection of Spanish credenzas and tables, as well as a squeaky, ancient plastic radio that ground out some unrecognizable Mozart in the name of atmosphere. Here the Master would make his drawings of me.

Right away, Dali asked me to take off all my clothes. This scared the living hell out of me until I sized up the very old man and figured that if he got worrisome I would be more than capable of fending for myself. Besides, I was going for that spot in the Louvre. So, off came the phony Chanel, the chains, the flattened pearl earrings, the works. I sat down, as directed, in a wretchedly uncomfortable neo-Spanish chair, and tried to look "cool." I was in a contest with myself to prove how sophisticated I was, and I was damned if I was going to be unable to handle this situation. This resolve came slightly unglued when I saw with horror that Dali was crawling under the table separating us. What was going on here?

Suddenly, down on the floor, out of my sight, I felt him begin to suck my toes.

I managed to mutter something about having to leave to walk the dog and, after throwing on all my clothes, slid out of there without betraying that I found this at all out of the ordinary.

I did, however, return to that little room for more "sketches," none of which I ever caught a glimpse of. I am not even sure he ever really drew me; I think it was even kinkier than that. But I was far too naïve to figure out what was going on. Was it anything more than a naked photographer's stylist waiting for immortality? One slide for Art History classes around the world?

Two final encounters persuaded me to abandon my ego plan as flawed. The first involved a session in what Dali called "The Cathedral"—his curious name for the entire floor of connecting ballrooms he had rented for the occasion. Across Fifth Avenue there was a church, Saint Thomas's, which, along with the streetlights in the snowy night, added considerable ambiance to Dali's "Cathedral." The only furniture was a hotel-style Madame Récamier couch, upon which I was duly arranged (naked, of course, and pretty cold). I was somewhat mystified when the Master produced a small florist's box containing three fat gardenias. I was directed to cross my ankles and stretch out my arms on the back of the sofa while he carefully placed two flowers between my fingers, and the other between my toes. Then, in a flurry of supposed sketches (which I tried in vain to see), he calmly pronounced: "There. Those gardenias are your stigmata, and *you* . . . are the Christ." He also mentioned that I was in good company, since Mia Farrow was Saint John the Divine.

I decided to end the sessions, because it was slowly becoming clear that the portrait was never going to happen. There was one final lunch, however, to which I and the other Dali characters were summoned, in a pretentious gourmet club near Grand Central Station. A dreary room had been set up with a dais flanked by two long tables. At the center was guess who, and around the U-shaped tables most of Dali's fantasy creatures were sprinkled amongst the regular club members in their tweedy attire. My lunch partner was a dull airline pilot who loved truffles and Grand Marnier. Each of us from the Dali collection had a "What am I doing here?" look on our faces as lunch began. I reached for the little round wheat roll on my bread-and-butter plate, and broke it open to butter it. There, in the middle, was a small soapstone cross.

That did it. I snapped the roll back together, leaving my "favor" inside, glared at Dali at the head of the table, and left. I knew I would not be playing with this crowd anymore. Several days later the Master called to ask me if I had enjoyed myself, and I was deliberately cold. He said, "But you were divine. That was the Last Supper, and, oh, how you suffered." Wacko.

Some weeks later, I was home in bed with raging flu when the Sokolsky studio called to ask if they should send over two enormous boxes of flowers that had arrived for me. I was too sick to get out of bed, so I asked the secretary if she would please put the flowers in water. Thank God. One box contained an enormous branch of pink cymbidium orchids. That was okay. The other contained something that would have given me a heart attack if it had arrived at my door: a full-grown live iguana with its long ratlike tail strung—poor thing—with imitation pearls. I had the creature messengered to a reptile store, and I closed the book on "How to Get Your Portrait in the Louvre."

And then there was modeling. Over the years a kind of myth has sprung up about my career as a Top Model, but the truth is, I could barely pay the rent on my earnings in that profession. Most of the time I arranged my body in some sort of contortion that I thought looked professional and "interesting," and then opened my mouth as though I were catching goldfish. The look was not a success. But once, when Sokolsky was doing an ad for Chanel, the account executive, Kitty d'Alessio, asked him if he would mind letting me take several days off to go to Puerto Rico so that they could use me for an ad they were shooting with another photographer. He agreed, knowing that I would make some good money. That photograph of me, naked under a huge waterfall, appeared in every drugstore in New York. Later, I did a lot of photographs as "the girl with the great job" for *Glamour* magazine, as well as some television commercials for Chanel and Polaroid. These jobs constituted the myth of my so-called modeling career, and it was not until *Goodbye, Columbus* was a big hit that anyone seemed particularly interested in the girl with the long straight brown hair and crooked teeth.

I was a junior at Wellesley when I first appeared in a magazine. *Mademoiselle* ran an annual guest editorship contest for college students, and the winners spent the month of June apprenticing as junior editors, an opportunity that opened doors in design, fashion, and journalism. I entered the contest with faint dreams of a career in the fashion magazine business, and to my amazement I won one of the coveted spots with my cartoons and drawings. During spring break I went down to New York for a preliminary meeting with the editors, and while I was there a staff photographer took my picture.

Several days later I had a phone call from their editor, Edie Locke, who said, "We're putting you on the cover." I was stunned. (It was some picture, too.) But suddenly, I found myself a bit of a celebrity—special, somehow, for having been singled out among college girls all across the country. That summer, Eileen Ford promised me a lucrative three months as a college-girl model. As it turned out, the job barely paid the bills when college resumed in September, but it did provide some dates with at least a few real jerks who normally would not have looked at me because I had no money and couldn't play tennis. They could say, "My date is a star."

There were plenty of problems with how I looked in those days, when, unlike today, there really was A Look. I was always too healthy, not pale enough, too bold in the eyebrow department to be considered a candidate for anything but the occasional fashion magazine modeling, which was far less lucrative than appearing in an ad. I was also terrified of the camera, a problem which I can now see clearly carried over to the movie camera later-on.

I never looked attractive in heavy makeup, and the way I put it on back then, thinking I had the professional model's touch, was a sight to behold: wing-tip eye shadow—maybe pearlescent—in the beginning, red lips, and later on, chalk-white mouth and overly blacked-out eyes. Daddy used to see me get off the train in my model regalia and he would be so horrified that I took to scrubbing my face clean in the women's room of Grand Central Station, like some hooker with a day job at a convent.

At the end of my years as a stylist for Melvin Sokolsky, a friend suggested I might like to join her one night a week at an acting class. That sounded like fun, and an interesting way for me to explore some of my inhibitions. At that moment I didn't think seriously about becoming an actress, but I did enjoy the classes, and I worked hard. I thought I would just let the experience unfold and see where it took me.

One day an agent saw the Chanel ad in a drugstore window and, tracing me to my job at Sokolsky's studio, asked me if I would like to audition for the part of James Coburn's girlfriend in a film called *The President's Analyst*. I was part of a cattle call, and it was definitely a long shot. I arrived at the set in a brilliantly striped micro-minidress, all legs and long straight brown hair. I rec-ognized several of the other women as models I had booked at Sokolsky.

The test should have been simple: just walk to the camera and back with as much Sexiness and Personality as possible, and then stand still for a close-up while a very gracious producer, Howard Koch, asked a lot of questions. Simple? Traumatizing. First, an old-time makeup man sat me in a chair and slapped a lot of makeup on my skin, aging me five years. Then he gave me some gooey green eye shadow under my John L. Lewis eyebrows. The effect was early Charles Addams, but maybe, I thought, that would translate as "movie actress" on film. I doubted it, and by the time I tried unsuccessfully to imitate the sexy, languid walk of Lauren Hutton and the other blond beauties, I knew I was done for.

"Next."

I HAVE ONE modeling memory that makes me smile. Shortly after *Goodbye, Columbus* came out to rave reviews, I was asked to pose for a portrait page in *Vogue* called something like, "People Are Talking About. . . ." I would be photographed by Richard Avedon. For years I had longed to wake up looking like one of those swan-necked, lion-maned beauties invented by Avedon for the pages of *Harper's Bazaar* and *Vogue*. I was beside myself with the fantasy of how he would capture me: with the look of one who would soon be going to some faraway exotic place in her own jet, perhaps carrying a satchel of sapphires for currency.

I arrived at Avedon's studio in the pouring rain, the street below overflowing with traffic and garbage. The only sounds came from the strobe lights popping in the big studio. I was wearing bell-bottom jeans and a man's shirt made for me in Rome; around my head I had tied a peasant bandanna, which became my signature as the year developed. Avedon took one look at me and asked me to step on a special mark on the floor which had been preset for portrait photography; he snapped a few tests shots and thought for a second. My head was dizzy with images of Babe Paley, Suzy Parker, Jean Shrimpton—and Ali MacGraw. Then, matter-of-factly, he asked me to go downstairs with him. He placed me standing in the gutter in front of the 59th Street Gristede's, a chilly damp string bean in the New York rain.

And that was my Avedon portrait for *Vogue*. I was crushed, but of course he knew better than to pretend I was, even for a second, swan-necked exotica.

B y the time I auditioned for the microscopic part in the James Coburn movie, my agent had already sent me on dozens of fruitless auditions, and I was becoming fairly certain that I had no future as an actress. Each time I was sent up for the part of The Girl, I was met with the same scenario: someone would look quickly through my portfolio of mediocre modeling pictures, snap it shut with a brief "Thank you," and I would be on my way. It made sense to me somehow. After all, I had barely studied acting, wasn't at all sure that it was what I wanted to do full-time for a living, and I knew that the streets were filled with drop-dead beautiful women—I had hired a lot of them in my stylist days. I didn't see how I could compete on any level, but even so, I let my agent send me out on auditions.

And one day I was actually hired—to play one of five

women who would appear in the title sequence of a short-lived Kirk Douglas/Sylva Koscina film called *A Lovely Way to Die* a.k.a. *The Pineapple Print*. It was my first film role, one day's work at New Jersey's Monmouth Race Track, where thousands of extras would fill the stands in response to radio announcements to be in a film with Kirk Douglas.

I would be picked up from my apartment, but I was expected to bring my own costume. The other four women all had breasts; I had legs, and that was about it. The immortal piece of dialogue I had to memorize was "Come on, sweetheart," which I was to scream at the top of my lungs in a close-up shot with "Mr." Douglas as his horse raced by below us. One or two takes should have done it, because it was probably just the background for the electricians' credit line.

They put makeup on me, approved my dress, perfectly straightened my hair, and then escorted me to the set, where I nearly had heart failure. I don't know how many people it takes to fill the Monmouth stands, but I am guessing tens and tens of thousands. On this day, they were all waiting to see Kirk Douglas, superstar. I was escorted to my seat in the middle of these excited fans, who were mostly women, as I recall. I waited with mounting terror for the star to appear.

Suddenly, there he was, wonderful-looking and charismatic, with rows of fans parting like the proverbial sea as he arrived. On his way down the aisle he checked his hair in a tiny mirror held by the makeup man who scurried along beside him. Finally, everything in place, someone called "Action!" My line squeaked out.

"Louder."

"Take Two!"

Once again I screwed it up. Now I could feel the panic and displeasure in the crew immediately around us. Who was this bimbo? Did she think she had a real part? I was mortified that I could not just belt out that moll-like line, but no matter how hard I tried, I was awful. Finally, however, it was done to everyone's satisfaction, and I raced off the set relieved and dying to get out of there. Kirk Douglas offered me a ride back to New York City in his big limousine, and I got an early picture of the difference between extra and star. But he was interesting and gracious and intelligent, and all things considered, I was lucky. I went back to the comparative simplicity and safety of my little apartment on West End Avenue, where I could walk my Scottie and not shout like a stevedore at the top of my lungs to a horse that didn't know who I was.

I always think of Washington's Birthday as being especially for children: no school, and a big cherry pie to commemorate a President who was so honest that he admitted he had chopped down a cherry tree. Amazing concept, that, in our political time. The innocence and sweetness of it just overwhelms me. Even if the story is apocryphal, I miss that in my sense of the twentieth-century world.

And I think that what I miss about the movies is that same innocence. When I think back over the films and television projects I have done in the past twenty years, I am saddened by the fact that I could never quite recapture the excitement and freedom I had when I did *Goodbye, Columbus*. Almost from the moment it began, it was fun and it was safe. I so trusted Larry Peerce, who directed the movie, and Stanley Jaffe, who produced it, and all of the cast, that I was not afraid to do or try anything. I think it may be my only sustained work on film in which I don't seem to be shrinking away from the camera, and it was during the making of that movie that I decided I wanted to become an actress.

I remember the first time I saw the finished film. I went with my agent to a little room at Movie Lab, on West 54th Street. It was two o'clock in the afternoon, on the 11th of March, 1969—so long ago. I kept a kind of ersatz journal then, with drawings, and on that day I sketched a long-legged young woman in bell-bottom trousers, crouched down in her seat in the empty screening room, hands covering her eyes. There was really nothing in my experience to prepare me for the sight of myself, so much larger than life, up there on the screen. I felt a combination of excitement and disappointment.

The fact that I was cast as the lead was, to me, pretty amazing. I had had virtually no acting experience, and, in the months that my agent had sent me out for dozens of parts, I had not had any luck. Which did not surprise me. One of my last interviews had been with a particularly repulsive well-known producer, and when he asked me to come back that night to his hotel room to "read," I decided I had had enough of the charade of me as an actress. I was looking for some other way to make a living when my agent called and told me that Paramount was making a film of Philip Roth's novella, and that I must go on one last appointment and meet the director. I had read Goodbye, Columbus, and I could see that the part of Brenda was complex. I thought it was pointless to go for the interview. But I met Larry Peerce, and over a period of weeks he had me do improvisations for him with different actors. Although I was surprisingly comfortable doing this, it seemed to go on for a long time, with no decision. Then one day the producer told me very tactfully that four couples were being tested in Hollywood, and I was not among them. I understood and was relieved; my acting career was finally over.

Five weeks later the phone rang and it was Stanley Jaffe telling me that the screen tests had not worked out, and would I please come in again, this time to read with the man they had signed to play Neil: Richard Benjamin. My initial, private reaction was, what was the point? But from the first reading with Dick, I had a vague feeling in my stomach that somehow I was going to wind up playing Brenda. I was right.

I had about two weeks before filming was to begin; two weeks in which to shuttle back and forth to Philadelphia, where my costumes were being made, and two weeks in which to come up with some semblance of a tennis game. Brenda was meant to be an ace player, and I am anything but. Every morning I spent the hour before rehearsals at an indoor tennis court, where an Australian pro tried to teach me the game. One morning he told me I was coming along nicely, that I "could be good." I asked him if that meant in ten days.

Much later in the summer, when we were shooting the twilight tennis game, my progress was put to the real test. The camera and crew were set up far away from the court, to record the scene as day slipped into night. The only sounds meant to be heard were the plop-plop-plop of the balls as they were lobbed over the net by two players going for blood. I kept missing the ball, and suddenly I heard, from what seemed a very long way

away, the sound man: "Brenda!! Will...you...stop...
saying...shit!"

FOR THE first two days of filming we did nothing I hadn't
already done for television commercials: it was all walking
around, no dialogue. I thought that movie making was
not such a big deal, especially with people as nice as the
ones working on *Goodbye, Columbus*. Then came a day
of terror. On the third day of shooting there was a nothing
little scene involving Brenda and Neil opening the front
door and running up a curving flight of stairs. On the way
I had to hit a few key spots for the lighting, and toss off
the line "Come on up: I'll show you to your room." I
froze. Thirty-one times.

It was a sweltering summer day, and about a dozen
members of the crew were stuffed under the curve of the
staircase to catch this remarkable moment on film. Out
of the corner of my eye I could see Stanley Jaffe pacing
back and forth, gnawing on his nails, as he is wont to
do. As the tension grew I got worse and worse; I wanted
to cry but didn't dare, as I knew it would destroy the
incredible amount of "natural" makeup I was wearing.
My mind raced, calculating how I would be able to pay
for the time I had cost them. I knew I would be fired
that night, and a new Brenda shipped in as soon as
possible. Who could blame them?

Larry and Dick took me outside for some air and spoke
soothingly to me, hoping I would relax. Then, just before
we opened the door to run up the stairs for the thirty-
second time, Dick kissed me, just as the character might
have done. I was so surprised that the door opened and

I was up those stairs, delivering the line before I knew what I was doing. Take thirty-two: print.

Brenda was a very bitchy character, with a family who behaved in ways I certainly never had seen my family behave. I was constantly screaming at my mother, who was played by a wonderful actress named Nan Martin. She was so aloof with me during the shooting that it wasn't until the last day that I realized her behavior had all been in character, that she, too, was doing everything possible to help me.

One day, during one of our ugly fight scenes, I went to Larry in tears; my nastiness had come so easily this time that I told him I was afraid I *was* Brenda. He said that all women have a little of Brenda in them. One of the great treats of this first movie was that I had been given a three-dimensional person to play, not one of the caricatures I would be offered later on.

While I was waiting around, hour after hour, for the actual filming to happen, I devised a way to keep from losing my mind. It was the period when everyone was wearing what they called "love beads": microscopic little Indian glass ones that you thread with a needle. I made dozens and dozens of strings of these beads as a way of keeping my mind on work and still not going crazy with boredom. It is not easy, after getting up unspeakably early, to sit in a makeup chair for an hour and then wait around interminably for filming to start. My solution got a little out of hand when the various heads of the different crews started coming to me for their "orders": ten for the electricians, seven for the camera, four for the props.

The crew is very important to me when I am working. The energy of everyone on a set is so interconnected that any bad feelings are felt instantly by everyone. I have always felt safe with a crew. My problem comes when the camera turns and a subconscious part of me feels exposed to the anonymous "them" out there. It is certainly not about people on the set; it is about the "them" who see the movie, I guess. In my worst moments, that is what shows on screen. But I trusted Larry Peerce and everyone connected with *Goodbye, Columbus*.

That included shooting several quick nude scenes, which were intrinsic to the film. I remember one freezing-cold night in particular, when we had to do a swimming sequence at the pool of the country club where much of the film was shot. I had to jump into the icy water over and over again, at about three o'clock in the morning. Between takes I was bundled snugly in big towels and electric blankets. In my cocooned deck chair I looked more like a pampered lady crossing the North Atlantic than a naked actress waiting for her hair to dry for another take.

The drive back to New York City after those all-night shootings was magical. We usually finished work just as the sun was sending out its dawn warning on the horizon, and before we jumped into our cars to go home to sleep, we ate tremendous breakfasts of eggs and sausages and coffee in the half-lit garden. Night shooting always exhilarates me. It makes me feel as though I belong to a special group of people—the ones who are allowed to stay out all night and play. It is as close to show business as I can get.

Because the reviews for *Goodbye, Columbus* and for me were so favorable, after it was released I would never again have the total freedom from expectation that I had with that movie. When it was over, it was as if a part of my life had ended.

However, the time between that last ice-cold shot of me swimming underwater (for the titles) and the release of the movie was eight months. During that time I had a very strange thought: what if no one goes to see it? Then what do I do?

I stayed busy doing my occasional modeling assignments and making a conscious effort to pay attention to every small detail of my daily life, as if in fear that these realities were going to be taken away from me forever. Suddenly the modeling situation was amusing to me, because word was out that I had done a movie, and I found myself a little in demand. I never had felt comfortable doing the work but I was grateful for it, because the notion of life as a working film actress had no reality for me yet.

I took acting classes, with a kind of desperation, because I had been signed by Paramount to do two more films and I didn't know a thing about acting. I did something very dangerous: I enrolled in both Sanford Meisner's and Lee Strasberg's classes, each a three-hour intensive session, twice a week, back to back. I would leave five minutes early from one class, just in time to slide into my seat at the other. If either of these gifted but egomaniacal masters had discovered what I was doing, I would have been summarily thrown out.

I remember one rather funny job interlude for a television commercial advertising some fiercely strong paper, which I had to *wear* in the form of a bikini photographed underwater in the Caribbean. The idea of going south at that time of year was wonderful, and the client even paid for me to go down to Nassau three days early to get a little color on my winter-green skin. That was nice, but I got a terrible sunburn on the second day, and then the weather turned frightful, and I froze every day thereafter. The clients waited in the warm sun on the diving boat, unaware of just how glacial it was down where I was working; the camera crew wore wet suits, but the only warmth I could get was from the generous cups of 150-proof rum that were handed to me each time I surfaced. Soon I didn't feel a thing. And miraculously, the paper bikini held together, dive after dive after dive.

The rest of the time, when I was not going to class or rehearsing for it, I observed the New York I loved so much. I was living in an updated railroad apartment on the Upper West Side, and every morning and evening I walked my Scottie along the same route. I noticed the face of each familiar character as I stood in line for Russian pumpernickel at our local delicatessen. I stared at a pretty redhead on the bus, and watched her later at the flower stall on 72nd Street, where the spring mimosa had been wrapped in bunches in bright-green paper, reminding me somehow of Paris.

I spent hours in museums. My favorite was the Frick, where I went every Sunday and sat in the atrium, which was filled with the overpowering scent of freshly planted hyacinths. There, for nothing, I could listen to chamber music, which was piped in from the concert hall next door. In a silent trance I revisited my favorite Corot landscapes on my way out. I took the long bus ride up to the Cloisters, where, overlooking the Hudson River and Manhattan, I could daydream in the winter-covered medieval herb garden. Some days I went to visit the shop of Anne Benjamin, on Third Avenue. I brought coffee in paper cups and strudel from the German bakery next door, and she closed the door to everyone else and let me play for hours with her antique clothes, which I collected and which she kept in faded lavender Bergdorf Goodman boxes.

I stayed home in a blizzard and drank hot chocolate and made decoupage valentines with my girlfriend Pam. Hers was for Michael Douglas. That was a long time ago. Sometimes I went to the Automat on 57th Street and watched intensely as a rather eccentric old gentleman managed his coffee cup and cigar while his silent, occasionally nodding, overcoated companions listened . . . and listened . . . and listened.

I needed the reassurance of the real details of my everyday life, as I felt increasingly that I was racing in front of a forest fire, and that this thing called Movie would change my life, whether I wanted it to or not.

With the arrival of March, the interviews came—little ones, but nerve-racking nonetheless. Already I worried whether I would be misquoted the next day, for all to read, in some silly little column in the *Daily News*. Nibbles were being taken out of my privacy, small at first, but threatening. One time I picked up the phone in my apartment to hear a strange voice: an agent in Hollywood who had seen a preview of *Goodbye, Columbus*, thought I was "fabulous," and was "sorry to have tracked down an unlisted number" but "could we do lunch?" I was shaken up: would there be no place to hide? I was introduced from the audience of the Ed Sullivan show, and it was probably then that it dawned on me that Hollywood was at least whispering at my window. It was exciting, it was scary; above all, it was foreign.

Things began to move very, very quickly; I was flown out to California, along with my agent and my boyfriend, the same young actor I was living with when *Love Story* came along. It cannot have been easy on him, having to hang around while I did a number of important interviews. I was also to be present at a screening of the film for the Directors Guild. I am glad I had no idea how big a deal that screening was—in my ignorance I could enjoy the experience of being put up at the Beverly Hills Hotel, star-style, and marvel at the price of a room-service breakfast with its strawberry-centered half grapefruit and single rose. A lunch was scheduled with the film critic of the *Los Angeles Times;* Charles Champlin had given all of us a glowing review, and it was a unique opportunity for me to sit with a critic who has not only always understood the details of the work, but has always gone to each movie wishing it well and hoping it will succeed. That lunch, as well as that review, are treasured memories of my early career.

I met Dorothy Manners, who was the last of a certain breed of Hollywood gossip columnist. She was very sweet with me and spent most of our lunch mourning the passing of the Golden Years of Hollywood, when actors were under contract to the big studios. The idea of being "owned" by a studio appalled me—that you would consent to be told how to look and where to be seen and with whom, all in exchange for stardom. She explained to me that there was one good thing about this system: that the same studios nurtured and prepared their stars, building their careers in a protected way. Today we are drop-kicked from our first financial success.

The Directors Guild screening, the main event of that first publicity blitz, is a Hollywood ritual for most major studio releases. It is a night of stars and lights and paparazzi, and the one for *Goodbye, Columbus* was no different. I sat in the middle of a nest of journalists, worried at first that they might not react at the right moments; but soon I forgot about them and sat there in the dark with my agent and some familiar friends from the filming, and felt enormous pride for us. As the lights went up, I took in the astounding list of names that paraded up the aisle to wish us well: the Henry Fondas, Roman Polanski and Sharon Tate, Jane Fonda with Roger Vadim, Anthony Quinn . . . it went on and on. And when Ingrid Bergman stopped on her way out to say she had enjoyed my performance, my evening was made. I don't remember much more about it except that Susannah York accidentally knocked into me, spilling red wine all over my too-expensive white silk dress. I took it as good luck, and sponged at the stains futilely with soda water, to the delight of the dozens of photographers.

Our evening ended at the now-defunct Daisy, a club that had been host to a lot of wild California times in the Sixties. We danced off some of the adrenaline of that evening, and stopped on the way home to devour tuna fish sandwiches and white cake with chocolate frosting.

I was right about one thing: my life would never be the same after *Goodbye, Columbus;* not the real world, not the movie world.

3

GETAWAY

I don't have a tremendous amount of Steve McQueen memorabilia around the house anymore. I have certain very special things: a Georgian silver teapot, and the alabaster *art nouveau* dancing lady—a kind of dazed Isadora Duncan, waving her gold-ringed fingers and pointing her perfect alabaster toes. Then there are the primitive necklaces Antony Powell made for the native costumes in *Papillon*: sand dollars and sea chestnuts strung on rawhide, hanging now on a bathroom door. Steve once said that I reminded him of a young racehorse or a greyhound, and I was heartbroken when someone stole the silver deco greyhound pin he gave me one Christmas. The surprise was that he had very good taste (he told me that once, of course). The presents he gave me over the years were all exceptional. Once, when I was remodeling our house, he brought home a beautiful printed silk robe and a hard hat. He thought I was tough and efficient and strong. And feminine. I loved the thought process behind that particular present. It was very sexy, very like him.

When I first saw him, the movie star "Steve McQueen," it was from a seat in the deep, dark Radio City Music Hall. The movie was *Bullitt*. It was one of the very rare times in my life, especially in my grown-up years, when I left the movie theater with my knees knocking for the star. Whatever it is that Star is about, Steve had it on screen. And, I was later to find, in a room.

It was more than the obvious electric-blue eyes and short sandy hair cut close to a perfect skull. He had a tigerlike quality. Something about his short athletic body reminded me of a wild animal, ready at an instant to pounce or attack. I think the essential thing about Steve was that he exuded danger. Lots of men and women are handsome or sexy, but it is hard for me to think of one film actor, except for Marlon Brando, who had Steve's innate mystery and danger. You never knew what he was going to do or say or be next. That translated on screen as excitement.

In life it was a little less romantic, making for a pretty nerve-racking home life as I tried to guess the mood of the day or the hour. He came by this sense of danger the hard way—by surviving a devastating childhood. And never trusting again.

Steve was born in 1930. He never knew his father, who abandoned him and his mother almost immediately. Later his mother, not able to deal with her wild young teenage son, left him at the Chino (California) reform school for boys, and went off to New York City to "find herself." Steve told me he didn't hear from his mother for months at a time—no birthday cards, no Christmas presents, no nothing—leaving him with a deep sense of abandonment. For the rest of his life he acted out his rage and distrust on all the women he met, particularly his wives. However, even understanding that history did not make it any easier to live with.

After Steve had spent several years in that loveless, terrifying jail, out of the blue one day his mother, then relocated in New York City, sent him a Greyhound bus ticket and a few dollars. Dressed in his lifelong uniform of Levi's and lace-up work boots, this sad and scared, tough and lonely young man arrived in Little Italy—the only blond for blocks. The combination of farm boy and street tough would be his image for life, costume and all. It belied a tremendous gentleness and vulnerability and real decency that it seemed to him wisest to cover up. Only occasionally did Steve dare to show anyone just how sensitive and gentle he really was underneath all the macho swagger.

I wish I had understood, then, all that I have since learned about alcoholism and addiction. Today, fifteen years later, it is clear to me that both of us were not only adult children of alcoholics, but we were ourselves carrying our own disease and not dealing with it. The pain of Steve's early life was a setup for the anesthesia he would need for the remainder of his days.

But now I see, too, that I was completely ignorant of the garbage I was carrying on my own back. It was easy to count the Old Milwaukee beer cans and joints in the ashtrays and come up with the obvious fact that Steve was somewhat stoned every day of our almost six-year relationship. What I didn't know then was that, whether or not I drank a lot during that time, I had my own illness. Alcoholism and the related addictions are not just the shot of tequila or the line of coke. Every single wounding childhood button that could be pushed by either of us was: Steve pushed ones in me that reminded me of the violence in my father, and I reminded him of his mother in ways that were intolerably painful. Steve loathed a woman who drank at all. That of course enraged me, as he was constantly drinking beer and smoking grass.

Because of the past suspicions and disappointments we carried with us, our relationship was doomed from the start. Steve tried halfheartedly to confront his problem through the help of an analyst. "Don't ever tell anyone I am seeing a shrink," he said. "I don't want anyone to think I am weak." He missed so many appointments that it was obvious he didn't really want to deal with the pain and history. At the same time, I was seeing an analyst. The doctor was a kind and decent man, but unfortunately his system consisted of listening to me nonstop for forty-five minutes while adding no advice or guidance whatever. I never knew what he was thinking.

With Steve and me, confrontation was the norm. During the horrible drama of my separation and divorce from Bob, Steve had to go to Spain to begin filming *Papillon* with Dustin Hoffman. I have always loved Europe, but as many times as I had been to Paris, I had never been there in quite the same emotional tizzy. Steve was a superstar in France and had recently been mobbed by fans as he walked down the street, so he had no particular desire to go there on his way to the Basque coast for

Papillon. But I was obsessed that we be in Paris together and behave like all the picture-postcard couples, holding hands and kissing along the Seine. As usual, I was high on fantasy.

Steve gave in to my wishes, and we checked into a tiny hotel off the Champs-Élysées, away from paparazzi madness. I had a favorite little bistro on the Left Bank and I persuaded Steve to take me there for dinner. It was all wonderful, and I was enjoying the ecstasy of being in Paris with Steve. This evening had the makings of another peak experience: I was in a city I loved, with a man I loved, and to tell the truth, there was a terrific rush that accompanied the stardom we both enjoyed at that moment.

We had a bottle of champagne and began to celebrate. We started to dance—and then something terrifying happened. Steve said, "Stop trying to lead."

Today I can see that that was quite a metaphor for our life together. That night in the restaurant I went berserk, began to cry and flail at Steve, who, incidentally, had a black belt in karate. We continued this scene outside in the courtyard, where only a miracle prevented us from being seen and photographed by some fan. When we got back to the hotel I passed out.

In the morning Steve told me quietly that I should go back to Los Angeles. I wept and wept and promised never to act like that again. Eventually he gave in, and we drove in tension and sadness from Paris to San Sebastián, on the Atlantic coast of Spain. By the time we arrived, everything was once again fine, but the experience had scared me. It was the first time in my life that I had completely lost control of myself. Years and years of rage and fear and sadness had been released by a relatively innocent sentence, and the situation was exacerbated by the amount of champagne I had consumed. (Later on, in analysis, I remembered an evening when Daddy was trying to teach me how to tango. He, too, had said, "Stop trying to lead.")

But I am jumping ahead. The Steve McQueen who leapt off the screen that night at the Radio City Music Hall was the same one who walked into my house when I was living in the Beverly Hills mansion with my husband, Bob. Steve had been preparing to do a film of a little paperback called *The Getaway*, about a bank robber and his wife: small-time Texas criminals, kind of romantic renegades. He wanted Paramount to consider doing the film, and he wanted "the girl from *Love Story*" to co-star with him (a potentially good idea at the box office). At the same time, at my insistence, Paramount had secured the rights to F. Scott Fitzgerald's *The Great Gatsby; I* was to play Daisy, the only film role I had ever longed to have. Funnily enough, the only actor I could imagine playing Jay Gatsby was Steve McQueen. So when he came over to discuss *The Getaway* with Bob and me, all I could think of was how to persuade him to do the *Gatsby* script.

Neither he nor Bob believed in the Fitzgerald story. I think they thought of it as being the esoteric whim of an artsy new actress from New York. (As it turned out, the eventual film of Gatsby did not quite work, so maybe they were right. Perhaps the lyrical beauty of Fitzgerald only works between the lines, in the mind of the reader, a kind of wistful elegy to a romanticized past. I don't know.)

The Getaway seemed to everyone to be the dream

package and the perfect career move for me. Steve was the biggest name in the business, and I was the star of the largest-grossing film of the year. My agent, my husband, and even the chairman of Gulf & Western, Paramount's parent company, were all desperate that I do the film. I did not want to; I had a year-old baby I wanted to be with, and the possibility of taking it easy and being lazy for the first time in my life. Besides, I did not particularly like the script, and thought I had little chance of being believable as the gangster wife of Doc McCoy, running from the law. I protested strongly, but finally backed down and agreed to go to Texas and do the film.

One thing that helped to convince me was the fact that Sam Peckinpah was directing. I remember our first meeting: I was in the pool, trying to teach my very plump and slippery child to swim. From the instant Sam stretched out his hand for a wet handshake, I liked him. As with Steve, underneath an almost caricature machismo was a most gentle, kind, and intelligent soul.

But the real reason I had hesitated was that I knew I was going to get in some serious trouble with Steve. There would be no avoiding it. He was recently separated, and free, and I was scared of my own overwhelming attraction to him.

What I chose to see in Steve from the very start was Survival. He was—even when our relationship was deteriorating badly—the person I would most choose to be with in a life-or-death situation. From a romantic point of view, I saw him as the one who would chop down trees to make the fire that would keep away the wild animals, the one who would pull fish out of the stream so that we wouldn't starve to death if we were marooned, the one to find the wild berries for a sugar rush. It went way past seeing him as the man who could fix leaky faucets. I knew that in any situation I would never be in fear and danger, as long as I was with him. If we had ever had the courage to be really honest with each other from the very start, I wonder what would have happened.

I was obsessed with Steve from the moment he stepped into my world, and there was never enough air for me to breathe to change that feeling. He was very taken with me, too, although I wasn't necessarily his dream lady, physically. I always felt insecure because of his attraction to blond models and *Playboy* centerfold types, who came at him by the hundreds. (At the memorial service for Steve, his first wife said wryly, "Steve liked to fuck blondes—but he married brunettes.")

Steve's attraction to me had something to do with my strength and education. He referred to me as his "New York intellectual," and he seemed proud of the fact that I had finished college, traveled a lot, and had some sophisticated times in my life. I am sure he was a little intimidated by some of that too.

If Steve had one glaring defect it was that he needed to have the approval of his small group of "yes men," people who worshiped him or were busy playing up to him in hopes of getting something. In a room of men who were his equals, though not necessarily in his field, he was incredibly insecure. He never ever realized that in a room of any group of people, he was the absolute center of attention. It could be subtle, but there was a perceptible energy—eyes cast his way, men's for one reason, women's for another. He was so intimidated and insecure, though, that he avoided socializing the way the proverbial native avoids the camera—as though it would have stolen his very soul.

The resulting isolation was hard on me, because sometimes I craved the company of stimulating people and of my own friends. We got the reputation of being hermits, barricaded "way out there on Trancas Beach, in Malibu," seeing no one but our two boys—Steve's son, Chad, and Josh—and the dog. My girlfriends were afraid to call the house, because Steve always sounded irritable when the phone was for me.

Once, several years into the marriage, Francesco Scavullo called to ask me if I would fly to New York to be photographed for his first book of the "world's most beautiful women." My ego and sense of desirability were so low right then that I needed to have that photo taken, that silly line of copy applied. Steve had made it clear that he did not want me to act once we were married; it was not in writing but it was pretty much understood, and my acquiescence to that wish had cut off my career at its very height. I felt like anything but one of the world's most beautiful women. Being in Scavullo's book along with Barbara Walters, Brooke Shields, and Margaux Hemingway would bandage me for a while, maybe even make me more desirable in Steve's eyes.

So I paid my own way to New York, ecstatic to be out of the house and on my own, back in "my" city. I arrived in time to do an interview with the *Vogue* writer who was doing the captions for the book, and then I had a bowl of pasta with an old friend. Afterwards we walked for blocks and blocks, catching up on our difficult lives.

I was just relaxing in my bed after a nice bath when the phone rang. It was 1:00 A.M.: it was Steve, calling to tell me over and over how much he loved me. As happy as I was to hear this, I was anxious to get a decent night's sleep to be ready for this photograph, and so I was relieved when Steve hung up. About an hour later I was startled out of my sleep by a pounding on the door, and to my surprise—and, frankly, secret annoyance—there was Steve, drunk and freshly off the late plane from L.A. The call had been made from a New York airport.

The first thing Steve did was to cross-examine me about who had been in the room drinking and smoking with me; while foraging for something to drink, he had found the glass and ashtray left by my *Vogue* interviewer. After we worked through that drama, he decided to make love, after which he passed out on the small bed, leaving me wide-awake with nowhere to go but the cold-tiled bathroom. Furious, I curled up under my cashmere shawl on the floor between the bathtub and the toilet and literally bored myself to sleep reading a book someone had given to me (about Freud, as I remember).

Luckily, the combined talents of Francesco Scavullo and the brilliant makeup artist Way Bandy produced two beautiful photographs of a huge-eyed, intense young woman with shiny hair, perfect skin, and high cheekbones. Hardly the weasel-eyed toad who walked into the studio that morning.

Why had Steve made this trip? It was not because he missed me (for three days), but because he did not trust me. Ever. In the crippling, claustrophobic mismatch that was our marriage, this was one of Steve's biggest contributions. For me, Steve was a symbol of success and power and fame without compromise of values. Today I think I needed to see him like that, to justify the panic I felt about the way I was living, the woman I was becoming. I was so attracted to my invention of Steve McQueen that I thought I could go off with him and learn to be real again. I didn't think about my family life back in Beverly Hills. Selfishly I just went on my way, rationalizing that I was saving my own life. It was as though I was operating outside of my own sanity and consciousness.

When I arrived in Texas for that first day of location work on *The Getaway,* I was met by Steve and Sam Peckinpah and driven back to the rented condominiums where the filming would begin. What a drive! Steve was showing off, and the first thing this ex-formula-one-race-car driver did was to spin the rented car in a dizzying loop across the four lanes of the freeway. It was a prophetic start to our relationship.

For the next three months of filming I walked the nasty razor's edge between occasional moments of sanity and remorse on the one side and, on the other, feverish excitement. Steve and I began our affair right away. I have a feeling that, with all the complications my own life brought to that relationship, he would have preferred it to have remained just that—an affair. On days when he was angry with me he would very flagrantly pick up one or more of the stream of bimbos who were always around the set, praying for a nod or more from Steve McQueen.

One night we went together to a small local party. Halfway through the evening, sufficiently loaded, he began carrying on with two local beauties right in front of me. I was livid, and left the party. Later that night Steve returned, and I could hear him in his apartment next door with the two girls. It was excruciating. The next morning he sauntered out onto his front step and casually asked if I wanted to come and make him breakfast. And the amazing thing is, I went in and cooked it. He had a kind of spell over me, with all of his macho swaggering. He liked to call me his Old Lady, a phrase I could live my whole life without hearing again. Today it conjures up an image of a steel-haired crazy woman on a Harley Davidson, out by the barn with some chickens running around and beer cans everywhere. No, thank you.

But for a while I found it sexy. Here I was, out in the wilds of Texas with the man's man of all times.

My best moments with Steve—the ones when the fantasy really worked—were when we were part of a kind of gang: Steve and Sam and some other super-macho groupies . . . and their Old Ladies. I liked being with the most important one, the star. As long as he seemed to love and admire me in that setting, I was ecstatic. I did not want to let on that they were seeing only a fragment of my personality, that I had a whole lot of things I wanted to be in addition to being his Old Lady. Stupidly, I took it for granted that those other things would be accept-able—even attractive—to Steve. But I was wrong. How many times did I hear him pay lip service to his "New York intellectual," when the reality was that this other side of me seemed to be anything but a plus in our relationship.

As a result, right from the beginning I never showed him who I was. I made up a kind of woman I thought would appeal to him, and I hid most of who I was. Dirty trick. It was the perfect setup for a ruptured relationship, after the early flirting had worn off and the ensuing rage and indignation had set in. A little voice inside of me began wondering, early on, "Why can't you see me?" I did not have the courage to speak up and say to him: "Look at me. Why can't you love the person I really am?" The answer was, and is, obvious: because I never showed him who I was.

With Steve, I learned the rules early. "Baby, you look great in jeans and a T-shirt." He said, "You have a great ass, but you better start working out now, because I don't want to wake up one day with a woman who's got an ass like a seventy-year-old Japanese soldier." That put the fear of God in me, and sent me scurrying off to exercise classes with my dancer-choreographer friend Ron Fletcher, with whom I worked obsessively four or five days a week for five years. And I've exercised ever since. Steve hated makeup and long nails. Dinner at the McQueen house was about feeding, not about preparing or creating food; it had to be on the table at six o'clock sharp. Early in the relationship I began to hate mealtime so much that I would prepare the dreaded meat and potatoes, serve it in front of the TV to Steve and the children, and then make something entirely different for myself to eat later on, by candlelight, alone, in a pathetic attempt to be "civilized."

But the fault lay with my initial campaign to win him, when the idea of sitting on the back of his Indian bike or in his new truck made me feel like the most desirable female on earth. I must give him credit: he never pretended to want to spend time backstage at the ballet or in the obscure parts of the Metropolitan Museum of Art or even on the streets of exotic foreign cities. By the time I met him, Steve had created a persona for himself that made him feel safe and comfortable, and he had no interest in anything outside that very specific world. I have always been adaptable to, even mesmerized by whatever is going on, whether it is a little gathering of the Hell's Angels or a black-tie dinner in London. It is all a huge adventure, and I expect the man in my life to be able to love it too. Few have been able to. Bob used to say that he "never ate a meal south of Forty-second Street" as a reminder that he was not interested in anything less than the first-class life. And Steve made a constant protest that he was just a simple man of the people who didn't go in for anything fancy. He seemed to close his eyes to the fact that he was treated, every waking second of his movie-star life, like royalty; and so his idea of "aw, shucks" simplicity had probably been flown in by special courier. He disliked my need to experience any of the cultured life, and only when we were being terribly Simple could he relax and enjoy himself. Only half of me was allowed to live; by the end of our marriage, the other half had almost died.

In the beginning, however, there were wonderful, romantic moments. During the filming of *The Getaway* there was that electric feeling you have when you are first in love—a kind of omnipotence and even madness that anyone within a fifty-foot range can feel.

At one point I had to leave Texas for the opening night of *The Godfather*. Bob, who had shepherded the film from its inception, asked me to be present, and Gulf & Western sent their private plane to the set after work on Friday. I was photographed ten thousand times being charming and loving to everyone, including Bob, when the real story was adultery in Texas. I felt like a piece of garbage.

By the time the movie was over, Bob and the whole

world knew what was going on, and I felt that I might be having a nervous breakdown. I took to keeping scotch—a drink I loathe—in the refrigerator, and drinking far too much of it in a vain attempt to block out the guilt. In a border town, between film setups, Sam taught me how to shoot tequila. I loved it, too.

Bob called, terribly concerned that I was literally cracking up. He said, "You need a serious break from all the insanity of this movie. I am going to have a car meet you at the airport and take you to Murrieta Hot Springs for two weeks of rest and babying. You need time to think, and I would like to send you where you can be undisturbed and come back to your senses."

I went, guilty about one relationship, infatuated in another, and utterly exhausted from the drama. I saw the time alone as a possible stay of execution. But alas, it was not that simple. The plan was for me to talk to no one during that time—to have two weeks, and more if necessary, to sort myself out.

I had a dizzying amount to think about, and although I hoped that my choices would become clear while I was sitting there in eucalyptus steams and salt-glows, I know that what I really hoped was that it would all just go away. I knew that I had stepped over the edge with my now-too-public affair, and that I had never bothered to examine the destruction I was causing in my own family. Besides the hurt and embarrassment I was causing Bob, there was the all-important issue of my son. My strongest memory of that time at the spa is of a numbness, a desire to have some decision made for me that would involve no one's getting hurt. It was a very passive attitude, a wish impossible to accomplish.

I told the switchboard a hundred times that I was not to be bothered by anyone. However, they were very intimidated by the power behind the names, and so I was hounded by both Steve and Bob. One time I was naked and midway through a soothing massage when an attendant brought the telephone to me, because it was "Steve McQueen for you." Steve said he missed me so much that he just had to drive by the spa for a quick secret hello on the street. A guard at the gate saw Steve's dark-gray Porsche 911 and told the telephone operator—who promptly phoned Bob.

The last straw came one afternoon when I was sitting in a tub of some funky therapeutic mud. I was nearly asleep when an attendant, almost swooning as she rushed into my little cubicle, announced that "[I truly cannot remember which one] is on the phone." I had had it; I checked out that day.

I went home, an emotional wreck, to Bob.

I am not sure how long I was home in Beverly Hills between the end of *The Getaway* and the end of my marriage to Bob, but it was hell for both of us. I was too tired and confused and scared to be really present for anyone but two-year-old Joshua. Because of my absolute obsession with Steve, I could think of nothing else but somehow being with him. Bob tried everything to keep me from blowing up our lives. Reliving the pain I gave him makes me sick. He lovingly said, "These things do happen, but I understand. I think if we go away together on a wonderful trip, to places you love, we can put all these terrible times behind us." He took me to the Hôtel du Cap in Antibes, because we had had glorious times there in earlier days, and he took me to my favorite city on earth, Venice, all to bring me back to sanity.

I was numb. I walked the beach collecting thousands of shells (mostly pink, like babies' ears) and saving them in a faded butter-colored damask napkin—for Steve. I wallowed in my melancholy and melodrama day and night. I sketched the Turkish minarets of the Excelsior Palace Hotel as though I were the only "artist" who had ever found Venice to be the most sublime place in which to weep about a love affair. I made furtive calls and wrote furtive letters and poems—to Steve. And one foggy day, when I was walking down the Lido, once again fantasizing that I was Isadora Duncan—just too uninhibited and creative and passionate to be contained—I bought Joshua his first shoes: two pairs of canvas sandals, one red, one navy, with white rubber soles. I still have them, and when I see them I feel very sad.

Nothing worked. When we got back from what should have been a cure-all trip, I was still living in "our" home, but the really tough, long days began. One night a family friend, a lawyer, came to the house for drinks, and he sat there gently trying to tell me why I shouldn't be behaving as I was. Something snapped. I was drunk, certainly, and I excused myself, went into the kitchen to use the butler's telephone (which had only one extension), and reached Steve to tell him I was leaving, that I was driving up to his place and needed help. Then I went back into the living room and asked the only coherent, if selfish, question of the evening: would I lose Joshua if I left, now? The lawyer said I would not.

I got into the brand-new convertible Bob had just leased for me, and tore out of our driveway, knocking over a statue and scraping a few cedar trees. When I arrived at Steve's house there were big gouges in the car and a patch of yellow paint where I had sideswiped a traffic sign. Steve took one look at me and booked a room for me in the Beverly Hills Hotel. Alone. That was probably the only cool move of the evening. I slept the sleep of the dead and got up in time for, of all things, an interview with *Women's Wear Daily*. Somehow, in a much finer performance than I gave in most of my films, I pulled myself together to do my charm for the press. I remember that I wore a Euro-trash trendy lavender shirt and pants, and an absurd new hat from some shop in Saint-Tropez. I hate the photograph, because it reminds me of that time. From then on events moved quickly. Candice Bergen, whom I had known only slightly through our mutual press agent, offered her temporarily vacant house until I could find a place for Joshua and me. From that moment, for her unending support and intelligence, whimsy and humor, Candy became one of my cherished friends.

At the time, Steve was living in a tiny rented guest-house in the middle of a wooded area between the San Fernando Valley and Beverly Hills: a secret hideaway with more flowers and gardens, real and painted and embroidered, than seemed possible. His landlady persuaded a neighbor to rent me their house, which was actually next door to Steve's. Because of the way the roads are laid out in that part of Coldwater Canyon, we had two totally different addresses, and our driveways were about four miles apart. Actually, our houses were separated only by a big field. Many were the nights that we would have some terrible row over nothing, and one of us would slam out of the house to Go Home. A half hour later we would find each other, inching across the field, each of us going to check up on the other. It wouldn't be long before we would be laughing at the melodrama of it all.

I have often thought, since then, that it is not a bad way to live: separate houses, each with its own stuff and eccentricities, no permission necessary to rearrange each other's treasures, no need to put some great-aunt's hideous grand piano in the living room. I think it may be a sexier way to live, too, with room for reconciliations.

But for me, such an arrangement would have to presuppose trust and monogamy. And come to think of it, maybe I would want the separateness only when I wanted it. (Is it any wonder no one can live with me?)

During my stay in that place, Steve left for Jamaica and *Papillon*. It was a difficult period for me. Bob had forbidden me to take Joshua out of the country, and Steve was the kind of man who could not go more than a couple of weeks without his Old Lady and not feel that he had been abandoned. So I shuttled between Jamaica and my newly rented home with my wonderful baby. I would have preferred to have been with Josh the whole time, but I was scared that Steve would get involved with someone else if I stayed away too long.

I was no good to anyone, and Steve did not help. I felt guilty and sad when I left Joshua, and when I got to Jamaica it was always several days before Steve would warm up and trust me. It was his way of keeping intact the brittle survival shell that kept him from ever again being hurt by a woman. And the shell would be on again a few days before I left, to ensure he was prepared to survive the next two weeks without me.

In between, we had some happy times, though. The

studio had rented Steve a typical Jamaican house with big mahogany ceiling fans and a garden filled with exotic flowers. There was a cook who prepared us native food and fresh fish every night—another way of saying "eighty-seven ways to cook red snapper." When we were not on the set we listened to music, took long walks in the woods and on the beach, and generally behaved like two people on a lazy honeymoon. Steve discovered the Jamaican beer Red Stripe, and ganja, and when he wasn't working he was very relaxed indeed. He put on some weight, which was amusing because the costumers had to give him bigger and bigger black-and-white Devil's Island prison pajamas so that he could manage to look somewhat skeletal, his clothes swimming on him. While poor Dustin Hoffman subsisted on half a coconut a day for the sake of verisimilitude, Steve lived a comfortable, easy life during that movie. On the screen the performances are equally good. (Sam Peckinpah once told me that if I ever wanted to learn what film acting was about, I should watch Steve's eyes in close-up.)

Henri Charrière, the real Papillon, came to visit the set once. He was quite a charming character, but with a huge ego. His famous Papillon tattoo was visible to all, hardly the brilliant-blue monarch butterfly it once was but now, with age and not so firm flesh, a trembling lavender moth. The sight of it almost cured my desire to have a tattoo, even after I had seen the stupendous floral work on one of Cher's cheeks as she bent in front of me in her white leotard in Ron Fletcher's class.

I did try once to get my own, very small, very discreet, very—I thought—sexy tattoo. Steve and I were in San Francisco. I felt that a little rose on my groin would be appealing to him (along with the tight jeans and my ability to sit on the back of his motorcycle and hang out with the guys). Very early on a Sunday morning, as we passed the famous sixties tattoo parlor of Lyle Tuttle, I decided to have my little masterpiece done. We climbed the stairs to a funny room, where three sailors on shore leave were already sitting in old barber chairs, lined up for some art. I explained what I wanted and we were shown a separate room where "ladies" could have their erotica done in private. I was quite excited, until I looked closer at the poor soul in chair #1 who was in the process of having an elaborate arm tattoo reworked. It was a series of women's names, connected and crossed out with vines and roses and curlicues: JUDY (no) SANDY (no) BETSY (no) WANDA (yes!). He was writhing and vomiting from the excesses of a late night. Suddenly all I could think of was how wretched the whole thing would look years later, when it reached the pale-lavender Papillon stage. Mine too. We ran back down the stairs and out onto the crummy street. End of my tattoo phase.

When *Papillon* was finished, Steve and I moved out to the beach just beyond Malibu: Broad Beach Road, Trancas. At the time, it was a quiet little dirt road running parallel to the Pacific Coast Highway, past an intersection that boasted two gas stations, a supermarket, and a honky-tonk bar. That was the town. Broad Beach is all sand dunes and a deep swimming and surfing beach, the houses not quite so close together as in the rest of Malibu—where you can guess the brand of barbecue sauce on the next-door grill. Trancas of our time was a wonderful getaway, even by Malibu standards. "Real" people lived there, in funny old summer houses that had been rented back in the days when Trancas was considered much too far to commute, and too unfashionable for summer.

Steve and I had the best of it: our children educated in the local public school, our dog free to roam the beach from one friend's house to another. Life was wonderful— tuna fish sandwiches and surfboards and bicycles, each child with a little core of friends, whose parents we also enjoyed.

The ocean was a big part of our lives. Steve's son, Chad, a terrific athlete, was obsessed with surfing, the status athletic activity of Malibu. I have wonderful pictures of this twelve-year-old boy staggering down the beach with an enormous surfboard, trying to catch up with his taller heroes. Eventually, after hours and hours of deadly serious practice, he got quite good, and for days on end the only time we saw him was when he came into the house at the end of a long, cold day, his cheeks brilliant red and his body miraculously warm in the infernal wet suit.

I tried winter body-surfing but it terrified me. When I was way offshore and realized I would have to navigate those enormous mountains of deep green water, I was paralyzed with fear. I did not try the sport very often, but in that athletic family I felt stupid that I couldn't manage.

There was one occasion when I did take a perfect wave on my son's boogie board. It was the ultimate summer California beach day, and I was tanned and feeling fine, out in the relatively mild ocean, playing. I was about to take a wave in when I saw three people walking down the beach. What stood out were their clothes—a kind of "what to wear to the beach" display: everything just a little too perfect and *Harper's Bazaar*. The woman in particular was something to behold: a kind of sailboat of billowing diaphanous white fabric, floating rhythmically down the beach; "Midsummer Reverie," a caption might have read.

By some miracle I caught that wave and rode it all the way in and up onto the sand, where, suntanned and bikini-clad, I landed exactly at the feet of the three people from Mars. Who were: three heavies from my agency, including, in the white robe of course, my own agent, Sue Mengers. For a split second she didn't recognize me, and a look of something like horror appeared on her face as she watched this beach bimbo on a Styrofoam board coming right at her. It was a stunt I couldn't have repeated if I had been paid $10,000.

ALTHOUGH Steve had made it very clear from the start that he did not want me to go back to work, at that moment, work was the furthest thing from my mind, anyway. All I wanted was what I imagined to be a typical family life. Deep down, I figured that if I didn't make a fuss about the career issue then, I could get my way later on. No point rocking the boat. We had plenty of tense times as it was, and although we had talked about getting married for the children's sake, the subject only came up sporadically.

One night we had a terrific fight. After we had both calmed down, Steve said, "Okay, Baby—if you want to get married, it's tomorrow or never. That's it."

Not exactly moonlight and roses, but pretty much in character. We made a weird plan to get married in Cheyenne, Wyoming, largely because the name sounded very cowboy-romantic and it was also far from the beaten track of Hollywood. We decided we could fly part of the way, rent a truck (what else?), and sneak into town with the children to be married by a local justice of the peace before anyone figured out what was going on. The night before, we checked into one of those basic avocado-and-orange, shag-carpeted Holiday Inns. Steve and Chad shared one hard little bed, while Steve's daughter Terry and I were in another. Josh was in a rented crib under the coat rack, a rather hyper two-year-old surveying us with a baby bottle half-full of celebratory champagne.

The next morning Terry and I, dressed identically in long-sleeved T-shirts and madras skirts, went to the local florist for some little nosegays to hold during the ceremony. Chad and Steve and Josh, who was still holding a bottle and staggering around in his Oshkosh overalls, joined us. The justice of the peace had been spending a happy morning on the golf course—happy until the shock of his special visitors' request reached him.

And that was that. I actually don't remember the split-second service, only how dazed I felt at being the wife of yet another powerful Hollywood man. It was another moment of unreality.

In the early days of our marriage we were both terribly happy playing at being a normal family. Chad came to live with us, together with a family dog who guarded both the boys with devotion and scared everyone else on that beach out of their socks. And although Terry preferred to live with her mother, she and her friends were often at the beach on weekends, particularly at the beginning. Our life style revolved around family and small town. I think we were both exhausted by the tremendous amount of tabloid attention we had received, separately and together; it was a relief to spend time alone and with the children, on the beach or on long rides in the canyons. We stayed to ourselves, which started the rumor that we had become hermits. At first I was only too happy to do all the mundane things all young mothers and wives do— I was not interested in anything except trying to make our marriage and relationship work, and I played cook, cleaning lady, "simple" woman to the hilt. For a while it worked, and we were happy.

Aside from our tendency to fight, the early warning that my marriage with Steve was going to have its rocky times was his insistence that I sign a prenuptial agreement, because, he said, his first wife, Neile, had taken an enormous amount of money from him when they divorced. Personally, I did not think that was true at all. She had given up a promising career as a dancer and spent sixteen years bringing up their two children and holding his hand through the early days of his career. She was incredibly fair, hardly giving him cause for his paranoia. But I was so anxious that nothing go wrong that I did not even discuss this with Steve. I was caught up in the fantasy that we were so much in love that divorce was not an issue. A part of me was hurt, though, because I felt that my own track record was clean in the alimony department: I had not asked for or received a cent from my first two husbands. Nonetheless, I signed the document prepared by his lawyer. I even signed it all over again, years later, when we were really rioting. I guess I just hoped the whole subject of divorce and alimony would go away.

Now that I am older and surrounded by the sagas of ending marriages, I have stronger opinions about alimony. If a woman gives up her means of financial support—her career—to raise children and support her husband's work, and the marriage ends, then she should indeed receive a fair share of her husband's financial means. This is only just recompense, and unrelated to the anger and revenge some women express in lawsuits against their husbands. I no longer feel, as I did when I was married to Steve, that the full-time job of housework and child-rearing should go unrewarded financially if the marriage collapses. In my case, I gave up my film career at its peak not just in popularity but in financial potential as well.

When Steve and I finally dissolved our marriage, he got our house and everything in it, down to the frying pan and salad servers. I kept the books and clothes I came into the marriage with. Even at the moment of sad divorce, I felt I had done something very noble and classy: that the great "they" would think I was just wonderful, not like every other vengeful ex-wife. Well, I am not vengeful. At all. But that gigantic gesture of abandoning my career and my means of financial support was stupid. On every level it was one of my more expensive lessons.

While we were married, although Steve was a diehard homebody, he needed to know that he could take off with me (in his truck, of course) at a moment's notice. Or stay out all night. Or bring ten people home for dinner. Luckily, I found a wonderful Frenchwoman to help me with the children—and to help me with my French. As it turned out, we rarely had anyone at the house, but Julia Juhasz has been my friend and assistant ever since, and I have no idea how I would have managed my unpredictable life without her.

As little as Steve and I traveled, we did manage to spend some great times in Big Sur. We both loved getting away at the last minute, throwing a few things in the truck and making the long drive up the California coastline. As the hours and miles passed we could feel ourselves relax; Hollywood seemed a million miles away. We always stayed at Ventana, spending our lazy days walking the deserted beaches and our nights soaking in the hot mineral baths by starlight. Big Sur seemed to be a throwback to the happy life style of the 1960s, with nothing more pressing to do than to marvel at the Pacific Ocean as it crashed against the spectacular coast, hundreds of feet below.

Once, on our long drive north, we stopped at an army-navy store to look for old junk; this was a favorite pastime. Steve discovered some ancient World War II army rations, and on one of our hikes in Big Sur the next day, he dragged them out. "Here, Baby," he said. "Try some of these. They're really good, loaded with vitamins." (And I wondered why he wasn't interested in gourmet food.)

One weekend when we were in our favorite apartment in Ventana, Steve told me excitedly that some of his Hell's Angels pals were planning a run through Big Sur. He was going to meet them at the River Inn and "hang out." Would I like to come? I preferred to listen to Mozart in our room high up in the redwoods, and I spent the afternoon embroidering antique buttons onto the sleeves of an Afghani ceremonial dancing shirt.

Steve came back to the treehouse that evening, enthralled. "Man, that was great with the Angels. You should have come. Every time one of us wanted another coffee or beer, one of their Old Ladies got it for us." Silently I thanked God that I had chosen to stay home.

That night we had one of the more bizarre suppers of my life. Besides the Hell's Angels, whom Steve had invited (and who turned out to be nice men), we had made plans to eat with two men we had run into at the inn: Joel Schumacher, now a film director, whom I'd known in New York, and Howard Rosenman, a producer—both very funny men. In addition there was Diane Von Furstenberg, smoldering away in her violet cashmere Halston, mysterious as could be. What a table! We all drank a lot of red wine and then threw ourselves into the hot tub. Later that night my bathing suit was missing from the wooden peg in the women's changing room. I always thought it was taken by one of those Angels' Old Ladies. She sure liked me a lot.

ONE OF the less successful, albeit well-intended, trips I took with Steve was a birthday present he gave me: a romantic plan in theory, but a fiasco in reality. Thinking we could have a very special time going overnight by ship from Los Angeles to San Francisco, Steve booked passage for us on the last night of what I think was a world cruise. We drove down the coast to Long Beach, where we were to board the cruise ship, whose name I have blocked out. It all felt very gala and exciting, until Steve noticed an army of law officers and guard dogs alongside the ship as it lay at the pier, waiting to sail its final twenty-odd hours to San Francisco. The dogs were pulling at their leashes, straining to do their job of sniffing out drugs. The ship had just come from the west coast of South America, and one hapless sailor after another was taken away, sorry, no doubt, that he had not left his Colombian souvenirs behind.

At the sight of the dogs, Steve panicked. He had, of course, brought along his own stash of grass. He grabbed the public relations officer, who was falling all over himself at the prospect of having some movie stars on board, and succeeded in getting us into our room with the grass undetected. For the next twenty hours we more or less stayed in our suite, because there wasn't another private corner on the ship.

People who have been sailing on a cruise ship, crushed together for weeks, have their own madness. This group had even shared some kind of ritual alcoholic baptism on the icy seas of Cape Horn, and by now they were totally wacko. There was no one who wasn't having his last twelve drinks in one of the bars, which were all over the ship; and when we took a little walk we saw more than a few sailors shoveling their Colombian treasure into their noses before flinging the containers overboard, in anticipation of more dogs in San Francisco. By nighttime we were certain we were on the real Ship of Fools. I have never seen so much drinking and hysteria. It was a nightmare. Partway up the coast I looked out of our little porthole and thought I saw our house; I longed to jump over the rail and swim for shore. By the time we reached San Francisco we were cranky and cramped and determined never to go on a cruise ship again for as long as we lived. Once again there were those dogs, and the toughest female cops I have ever seen. This time Steve took no chances, and flushed what remained of his grass down the toilet. We raced for the airport and the quick flight home, where we were thrilled to find ourselves, our children, and our dog. So much for our romantic birthday outing. Still, it was a very touching thought.

One summer on Broad Beach, Steve came back to the house after a long walk with the dog to tell me he had just talked to Ronald Reagan, whom he knew from Republic Studios, where Steve had played in the series *Wanted Dead or Alive*. Reagan, recently out of a job as governor of California, was spending the month on the beach with Nancy and some state troopers. What a sight it was—the ex-governor's wife sitting very conspicuously under a big beach umbrella, embroidering, while uniformed men stood a few feet behind her, their arms folded like Smokey the Bear's.

I suggested to Steve that we invite them to our favorite local haunt: the Old Place, twenty miles into the Santa Monica Mountains, in the middle of nowhere.

The Old Place is owned by the Runyons, lovely, eccentric old-time Malibuites. She is an artist, and he cooks the best steaks I've ever eaten. He buys them retail at the local supermarket, where, if you're not lucky, you can find yourself stuck behind a shopping cart piled high with $600 worth of meat. Salad is three-bean salad from a can, bread is so-so, and the wine is atrocious, unless you bring your own. The Old Place attracts an incredible cross section of locals, from certain macho film industry types to the jumbo-hair-roller contingent from the Valley. The local cowboys and bikers all go there, as well as a regular group of misfits, providing great spectator sport.

This was the place we chose for the Reagans, to save them from some black-tie dinner in Bel Air, we thought.

We arrived early, took our booth, and ordered drinks. Suddenly, in through the swinging wooden door burst a woman with tremendous breasts wearing a black T-shirt on which was printed BEAVER. She stopped dead in her tracks when she saw us and said in a loud voice, "Holy shit! There's Steve McQueen and Ali MacGraw and Ronald Reagan."

I ordered some more bad wine and figured there was no way to save that evening. The Reagans were very gracious, but I doubt that the Old Place made it onto Nancy's top twenty restaurants list. We never were invited to the White House.

The last time I was at the Old Place, Tom Runyon still had the photographs from *The Getaway*—John Bryson's black-and-whites of Steve and me in a very happy, loving moment. It made me sad to see them, it seemed so long ago.

There are blocks and blocks of time from my marriage to Steve that I cannot remember in any detail. My sense of it today is that we would go along peacefully for days on end, and then suddenly find ourselves in a horrible fight. It must have been awful for Josh and Chad, who had already each survived one divorce. Our worst fight resulted in Steve inadvertently backhanding me on the forehead, breaking open the skin next to my eyebrow. Both of us were so shocked by the incident that it actually served to quiet us down for a while. After that encounter Steve was so upset that he decided that every time we had an argument it would be "safer" for him to go into town to spend the night. I had a healthy fear of Steve's temper and of his physical strength, and, while there is no way I would ever have provoked another incident like that one, there were times when Steve would get so angry that I was afraid of him, at least for the instant.

At this point in his career he was in a position of tremendous power and, together with Barbra Streisand, Sidney Poitier, Paul Newman, and Dustin Hoffman, had formed a production company called First Artists. Each actor was allowed to do three productions of his own choosing, and one of the projects Steve wanted to make was Ibsen's *Enemy of the People*. The studios were not crazy about that idea. They wanted to count on the predictable millions from a Steve McQueen action/adventure picture. They gritted their teeth and prayed the masses would go to *Enemy of the People* thinking it was another Western. The work involved in this classic was intimidating and intense, and it coincided with our remodeling our house.

The house was so torn up that it was all but impossible to find peace and silence in it for the duration of the filming of *Enemy of the People,* so Steve was rarely there. He came back for weekends, however, and I remember being crushed that he never noticed the tremendous progress made each week. I think that all my frustrated creative energy went into that remodeling, and I was starved for praise for what I was doing.

I was also avoiding what my sixth sense told me was going on in the big *pied-à-terre* Steve had rented in the Beverly Wilshire Hotel. It had made me crazy to know that he had put almost $50,000 into decorating it, and that the same couple we had caring for our plants at the beach also went into the hotel suite to take care of Steve's plants there. They were very cool and very loyal; whatever they saw, they never told me.

After we divorced I was told by more than one friend who stayed at the hotel that Steve's room, right next to the pool, was the scene of a constant parade of models and starlets. Sensing that, I never set foot in that hotel apartment. But the truth also was that I was secretly relieved to have him out of the house, to be alone with the boys as I worked on remodeling our home.

Our relationship began unraveling faster and faster, and more than once we discussed divorce. The subject always made me cry. I felt as though I had failed myself and everyone once again. One time I packed my suitcase and walked out the side door down to the beach. Steve saw me and, sad and upset, persuaded me to come back.

In spite of the fact that we loved each other enormously, the situation was doomed by phantoms of the past. Love was not enough.

In addition to the ongoing tension, something very distressing happened. One day between setups for *The Towering Inferno,* I was sitting with Steve on the lot at 20th Century-Fox when I looked down to see that I was in a pool of blood. Steve was terrified, and rushed me to the nearest hospital. I had had a miscarriage; I never even knew I was pregnant. It was very disturbing, and Steve in particular was upset. He always felt that if we had a child, we could save our marriage.

Alas, I don't think so. We were headed for a terrible collision, and having a baby would only have created one more child whose foundation would be severely rocked, as our children's had been.

Sue Mengers took me to lunch at the "in" restaurant, Ma Maison. She seated me in a particularly showy corner of the room so that the film industry could see for themselves that I had not died in those five years. She told me that Sam Peckinpah had made an offer to use me opposite Kris Kristofferson in a film called *Convoy,* named after a country-and-western hit song of that year. I remembered having read the script when it had been submitted to Steve, years before. I had loathed it, and I told Sue so.

She said to me, "Honey, your marriage is in trouble, you have no money, and you better take this job before it's too late. You haven't worked in five years, and you're lucky to get the offer." (Nice, warm, practical words, a version of which I would hear from her again when I balked at doing *Dynasty*.) Sue's candor is as legendary as her outrageous wit, but she has always been concerned above all about the financial security of her clients—and of me in particular. From her perspective, her advice was right: go back to work in it-almost-didn't-matter-what, with a director I liked and respected, and the hottest male star of the minute. (Kristofferson had just made every woman in the country roll over and swoon in the latest version of *A Star Is Born*.) Sue, who has been my close friend for years, wanted to force me to go back to work, for my own sake; as tough as her speeches sounded, she was usually right.

I went home to tell Steve that I had been offered this script, and that I would probably do it. He was sitting in a chair, nursing a beer. He turned to me and said, "In that case we are filing for divorce."

For once, I didn't cry or get hysterical. I pointed out that I could no longer afford to turn down work. With our marriage in such obvious trouble, I had to take the part, no matter how bad it was, to reestablish myself as a working actress. I pointed out that I had now signed his prenuptial agreement two times, and that if we did get divorced, I would receive no money from him and would soon be broke.

Steve offered to pay me a lot of money not to go back to work, but I not only distrusted the offer, I also knew that part of me was dying from not working. I saw no way to win, and so with considerable misgivings about the project as well as the future of my marriage, I set off to New Mexico to begin one of the nightmare jobs of my career.

I was sick about having to leave the boys, and I remember telling them: "Work is part of who I am. And one day you are going to look across a room and fall in love with some woman, and part of what will be special about her is that she works."

I prayed for a location that would speed the filming along quickly and pleasantly, in spite of a terrible script. (This should have been my final lesson in "You can't fix a bad script even if you are all so smart." But it wasn't.)

From the very start this location was a study in drugs, alcohol, and insanity, and I was certainly a manic participant. The cast and crew were pretty much divided between cocaine and tequila (or champagne, if you were Sam) on one side, and pot and beer on the other. I belonged to the former group, and I guess I thought I was some kind of terribly exciting man's woman. I had cut off all my hair, the stereotypical gesture of a woman who wants desperately to change her life. Unfortunately, my choice of a haircut, all frizz, dye, and permanent, grew less and less attractive with each month in the broiling Southwest desert sun.

The nature of this epic western—which featured two hundred eighteen-wheelers like a posse of dinosaurs—was that there were never less than hundreds of teamsters, would-be country-and-western singers, and movie groupies gathered wherever we were shooting. And usually what we were all doing was waiting for Sam to emerge from his trailer with a new and incoherent version of the pages to be shot that day. I did a small amount of cocaine, deluding myself that I was in control of my performance, but there was a kind of hysteria about the location that fed my escapist fantasy. We drank, we fought, we got high, we got crazy, and we slogged along.

Once, when I least expected it, Steve came down to location, which cannot have been easy for him. I went to Albuquerque to meet his plane, and as the door opened and the stairs were pushed up to it, I saw a tiny, down-vested boy lead Steve and the other passengers out of the plane. I was overwhelmed with emotion. I hadn't known he would bring Josh, and at that moment I fell in love with Steve all over again.

We had a month's break in the filming of this nightmare, while Kristofferson fulfilled some previous concert commitment. I was delighted to be safely grounded again in my home, with Steve and the boys. I prayed that the film, by now way over schedule and over budget, would be shut down so that I would never have to go back to New Mexico. Unfortunately, the film was not canceled, and I returned for a final ghastly month.

I have often wondered if making that movie was worth it in the overall scheme of my life; certainly it was the last straw in our crumbling marriage. But at least I had some money when the end came.

The crooked tooth and big eyebrows that couldn't get me arrested as a model—until *Goodbye, Columbus* was released (ART KANE)

(ABOVE LEFT:) My mother
(BELOW LEFT:) Daddy in his thirties
(ABOVE RIGHT:) At two and a half
years old
(BELOW RIGHT:) My younger
brother, Richard, was my great
playmate when we were growing
up in the country.

(LEFT:) Me at about ten: long legs and big feet
(ABOVE:) My parents made the silver oar pin I wore as a perfect little eighth-grader.
(BELOW:) My senior portrait at Rosemary Hall: four years that changed my life forever
(HARRIS, NEW ROCHELLE)

(RIGHT:) The Chalfonte-Haddon Hall float in the Miss America pageant of 1955 was the peak of my first "normal teenage summer": boys, beer, and this newspaper photograph to curl my parents' hair.

(BELOW RIGHT:) This cover and my guest editorship at *Mademoiselle* launched me into my first real job, as a fashion assistant. (LANDSHOFF, COURTESY MADEMOISELLE. COPYRIGHT © 1958 (RENEWED 1986) BY THE CONDE NAST PUBLICATIONS, INC.)

(BELOW LEFT:) All business and efficiency as I strode up Madison Avenue in 1960

Mademoiselle

August

50 cents

College 1958

(RIGHT:) Melvin Sokolsky, my soon-to-be boss, took this picture of me for my first wedding. I thought I looked like a Velázquez. (SOKOLSKY)

(BELOW:) In Paris for the collections. Melvin Sokolsky, center, and his brother Stanley (fourth from right): family for six years, friends for a lifetime (SOKOLSKY)

(RIGHT:) This photograph, taken in a Puerto Rican waterfall while I was still working as a stylist, appeared in drugstores everywhere. An agent saw it and asked me if I'd like to be in the movies. (JERMOE DUCROT, COURTESY OF CHANEL)

(BELOW:) Here with my invaluable co-star, Richard Benjamin, in *Goodbye, Columbus*: the first and only time I ever felt safe in front of a camera (GOODBYE, COLUMBUS COPYRIGHT © 1969 PARAMOUNT PICTURES CORPORATION AND WILLOW TREE PRODUCTIONS INC. ALL RIGHTS RESERVED.)

Courtesy of Paramount Pictures

National No. 1 Best Seller...

LOVE STORY

by ERICH SEGAL

(ABOVE:) An ad in a Hollywood trade paper announced the movie made from Erich Segal's blockbuster book, which put me on magazine covers all over the world.

(LOVESTORY COPYRIGHT © 1970 PARAMOUNT PICTURES CORPORATION. ALL RIGHTS RESERVED, *TIME MAGAZINE*, © 1971 TIME WARNER INC., REPRINTED BY PERMISSION; *LOOK*, PHOTO BY TONY VACCARO; BILL KING FOR *HARPERS BAZAAR*)

(LEFT:) Courtship days with Robert Evans of Paramount, for whom I did *Goodbye, Columbus* and *Love Story*. We married between the two films.

(RIGHT:) The Royal Command Performance and publicity blitz for *Love Story* took Bob and me away from our month-old son, Joshua. (PETER BORSARI) (BELOW:) The Evans family on Academy Awards night, 1971. Eight of us from the film were nominated.

I was always secretly hoping the fashion photographers would reinvent me as someone really glamorous. Once in a while someone did.
(ELISABETTA CATALANO FOR VOGUE ITALIA)

(ABOVE AND RIGHT:) I fought doing *The Getaway* because I sensed from the minute I met Steve McQueen that I might turn my life upside down for him. And I did. (JOHN BRYSON)

(LEFT:) With our director, Sam Peckinpah (MEL TRAXEL)

(LEFT:) A neighborhood
Easter egg hunt was held
every year in our back-
yard: Trancas Beach in
Malibu. (NICK RODIONOFF)
(BELOW:) Our very un-
Hollywood wedding, in
Cheyenne, Wyoming,
with Joshua, and Steve's
two wonderful children,
Chad and Terry

With some of my leading men:
(RIGHT:) Kris Kristofferson (and
trucks) in *Convoy* (JOHN BRYSON);
(BELOW:) Dean Paul Martin in *Players*
(© DAN BUDNIK 1991; WOODFIN CAMP &
ASSOCIATES);

(RIGHT:) In London for the opening of
Players: miraculously, Bob and I became
even closer friends in the years after we
divorced. (PIC PHOTOS)

(ABOVE:) The famous fight
scene from *Just Tell Me What
You Want* with Alan King
(PHOTOFEST)

(RIGHT:) In Venice with Robert
Mitchum for *The Winds of War*
(JIM GLOBUS/CAPITAL CITIES/ABC)

For almost ten years Josh and I lived in a rented house in Malibu where much of our life was as "normal" as I could make it.
(LEFT: JOHN BRYSON. ABOVE: WARREN ARNOLD)

(TOP:) Candice Bergen took this photograph of my mother and me.
(MIDDLE:) With Sue Mengers and Candice Bergen at lunch: friendship is almost everything.
(RIGHT) Mayor MacGraw (!) participating in the fight to save the coast
(KEN LEVINE)

(LEFT:) With Josh in 1990
(STEPHEN SIGOLOFF)

(BELOW:) With Adam and Caboose on our beach: two of my many animals—tonic for a lifetime (JOHN BRYSON)

The film came out to terrible reviews. When Josh and my mother came to the Directors Guild to see *Convoy* they were at a loss for words. Josh invented a dreadful country-and-western song—particularly bad, as he always loathed this kind of music: "My mother did a film called *Convoy*/What a piece of shit/She looked terrible/ It was terrible/What a piece of shit."

I came back from the final filming, praying we could bury the past and live happily again, only to find that Steve had left that morning to drive up to Idaho. Later I learned he had been having an intense affair with a brunette model whom he had "interviewed" in the bar at the Beverly Wilshire Hotel for a role in a fictitious film. Reflecting, I realized he had mentioned Barbara once before in passing, saying, "I met the most terrific girl last night. She just sits there and doesn't say a word." I should have realized then that I was in trouble, but I was too wrapped up in my own drama.

When Steve got back from his mysterious trip we decided to drive to Montana, to try to get our lives back on track. It was tense at first, with every conversation and every embrace accompanied by a question about my fidelity while I was on location. From my experience with Steve on that weekend when I had flown to New York for the beauty photograph, I knew that his at-first seemingly casual questions could turn into a kind of Nazi-esque grilling. The truth was that I had had a kind of druggy affair periodically during that movie, but as it was now common knowledge that Steve had been living a flagrantly free life for some months, I thought that if I did not go into my escapade, the whole mess of our lives might blow over and offer us a fresh start. It seems a sad testimony to our relationship and to my fear of his rage that neither of us could really be honest at this critical moment. We shoved the garbage under the table for the moment and, in a truck, drove to a little town in Montana.

Paradise Valley in 1978, before Elizabeth Clare Prophet and her disciples got there, was a sanctuary for renegade artists and writers. Part of me thought that if only we could pick up our family and live there, we could make it. Sam Peckinpah had a house nearby, along with Peter Fonda, Richard Brautigan, Tom and Laurie McGuane, and Russell Chatham; it could be a fresh start.

There was a real estate broker who knew everyone, and he asked if we would like to accompany him for a day and a night deep into Yellowstone Park, to a gentlemen's hunting lodge that he was responsible for checking on every so often. We would go on horseback. I am slightly afraid of horses, and therefore not much of a horsewoman, but I was given a very quiet, sweet animal along with a long yellow slicker to wear like the Marlboro Man, and off we went. It was one of the most spectacular days I had ever spent—just the three of us on our horses, alone in that magnificent national park with only a solitary fisherman and a group of elk to tell us we were not the last living creatures on earth. We had all four seasons: clear, brilliant autumn sunshine, which shone through the aspen leaves as though through a stained-glass window; then rain—cold, torrential rain out of nowhere. It snowed, too, just as we came upon a tent site where some hunters had pitched shelter. I remember thinking I had stepped back in time, into a kind of *McCabe and Mrs. Miller* scenario, where men in colorful cold-weather gear crouched over fires to keep warm and dry, and offered us camp coffee in speckled blue tin cups.

We rode out of the camp as the sun was breaking through again. I deliberately held my horse back so that I could not see the two other riders, and could pretend that I was all alone in the wilderness, thousands of miles away from home, and decades removed from my real and troubling life.

After a few hours we arrived at the lodge, where we would spend the night before riding back. What an astonishing sight, tucked way back in the middle of nowhere! A small cabin entirely filled with trophy heads and antlers—antler furniture, antler chandeliers, antler railings around the sleeping loft upstairs. Because it was already late in the season, everything was covered in white sheets, like ghostly dancers come to a frozen halt. The pantry was filled with real crystal and real silver; these fourth-generation WASP hunters from the East knew how to rough it when they took the train out to the Wild West to pretend, two weeks a year, that they were Teddy Roosevelt.

Steve and I had the little guest room, and we spent the night feeling we had journeyed back into another time and other values.

The next day we rode back to town, the way we came, through that ravishing wilderness, and then back to reality—Los Angeles. The storm in our relationship seemed to be subsiding. We had our last meal in Montana at a funky bar/restaurant, with our guide and a South American big game hunter he had befriended. At dinner Steve went on and on about trucks and camshafts and God-only-knew-what car talk with our guide. And I, having nothing to add to that conversation, decided to practice my so-so Italian with the other member of the dinner party, who seemed to be equally bored with the topic of vehicles. The South American was attractive and spoke several languages, but I had no interest in him other than passing the evening.

I had fallen back in love with Steve during our Yellowstone adventure, and I was looking forward to going home and beginning again. But, once again by ourselves in the hotel room, Steve started a jealous, rather sinister diatribe, and he did not let up all the way back to Los Angeles. He was convinced that I had been flirting with the man from Chile, and nothing I said could convince him otherwise. It was a nightmarish interrogation that went on relentlessly. I was exhausted from crying, and began to think that he planned to get me so tired and incoherent that I could be gaslit into saying what he wanted to hear: that I had been carrying on with whatever-his-name-was, in a "foreign language," deliberately trying to make a fool of Steve. It was sick and horrible. And it continued the next day, at home. There would be a lull for an hour or so, a suspected truce, and then he would start in on me again, like the Inquisition.

Finally, I snapped. I remember the look of horror on Chad's face as I screamed at his father that I wanted a divorce, and that I wanted him out of the house. (Steve, at least, had somewhere else to go.) I told him I would need thirty days to find a home for myself and Joshua, and that until then, he could come back to Trancas two nights a week to be with the two boys. I shouted so loudly that it was as if I were hearing someone else say the words. I was beside myself with rage and exasperation and defeat. And I meant it. As the words came out of me I felt an odd wave of relief that I would at last be out of the nightmare.

I had no idea where Josh and I would live. I wanted my son to be on the same school bus and in the same neighborhood so that he could see Steve and Chad and the dog and be uprooted as little as possible. It would not be easy though, as I had comparatively little money, and everything in the house belonged to Steve.

While decorating our house I had bought a number of Navaho and other tribal rugs, because I had always loved exotic textiles. Without asking me, Steve had automatically reimbursed my checking account for them. He now told me that I could not buy back two of them because "we [he and Barbara] will need them."

After weeks of searching, I found a house that suited all my requirements. It was a shambles, but I knew that with work I could make it into something that would be home. (In fact, *Architectural Digest* wound up photographing it and using it in their ad.) Shortly before we moved in, I called Steve on an impulse to tell him that I thought we had made a terrible mistake. His reply sent a dagger through my heart: "I am not in love with you anymore," he said. "I love you, but I am not in love."

Although I had asked for a divorce, I do not think the finality of our separation hit home until then. I cried hysterically, alone and out loud, with only the family dog to console me. Then suddenly, a miracle: I was out of tears. It was over. I had survived. I was ready to begin my new life, free.

I did not see much of Steve after that. Fortunately, I never ran into him at the market, or even on our street.

During the weeks right after we separated, when I was living like a transient with one friend or another, Sue Mengers asked me to come to one of her parties. These were famous, and for me, altogether terrifying evenings in the purest old Hollywood tradition. Everyone who was anyone gathered in Sue's eccentric Tony Duquette house, not only for her style and sense of humor, but also because it was *the* place to be in the Seventies. The mix of people ran all the way from established superstars like Warren Beatty and Julie Christie to whoever was the brand-new flavor of the month. I guess part of the reason we all went there was to be seen and counted—praying all the while that our slip straps were not showing. At this particular moment Sue felt that I should, indeed, be seen, to prove to the great "them" that I had not turned into the weirdo Malibu hermit the papers liked to label me.

So I put on some look-at-me outfit (thigh-high boots, tights, and a shirt designed for d'Artagnan) and threw myself into the lion's den. I was single now, Steve McQueen's ex-Old Lady, and a good catch for the piranha. I was so unused to being treated as beautiful or desirable that I was a sitting duck for two of the biggest lady collectors in town. I was "entertained" (that's a good euphemism for it) by both of them. Poor me, I thought then. Poor them, I think now. I had felt locked up for so long that I was anything but a casual, amusing date, and with these two, I was in way over my head. I like them both, as it happens—they are bright, and funny and sexy—but they were hardly mesmerized by the prospect of dealing with someone in my condition.

I remember on the final morning of my quasi-liaison

with one, I was sitting in my unfinished house, frantic because my car had just died and I was stranded, with too much to do. I will never forget how the minutiae of my lament turned him off. I was no longer that Hot New Single in Town; I was just a frazzled mother with tedious problems.

After Joshua and I were settled into our new house and had found a new rhythm, I felt I could go back to work on a more regular basis. In fairly close succession I made two films on location—the first, *Players,* in London and Cuernavaca, Mexico, and the second, *Just Tell Me What You Want,* in New York City. While I was away Julia stayed in the house to take care of Josh and our growing menagerie of cats and dogs. In between films I had quality time at home, grateful that for the first time in five years I felt my power and strength and some measure of peace.

In addition to the challenging work I had several wonderful love affairs, refreshing contrasts to the tension and claustrophobia of the last years of my marriage to Steve. One man, whom I met quite soon after we separated, had terrific children who were great friends with Josh, and what I remember most about that relationship is how much we laughed. It was just what I needed after all that sad time, and we have all remained good friends.

When I went to New York to do *Just Tell Me What You Want,* I fell in love with my talented co-star, Peter Weller, and our relationship seemed to be perfect just as long as it was long-distance. I could put in weeks of suburban motherhood in California and then give myself the "reward" of a fabulous week in New York, with all-night theater and music and dancing and conversation and romance; if the affair was a little unrealistic in some ways, it, too, paved the way for an enduring friendship. In every way I was feeling like a success again.

Shortly after I came back from filming in New York, Steve called. He asked if I would like to drive to Santa Paula with him to see the home and airplane hangar and planes that he and Barbara had bought. She was on a modeling job somewhere.

It is funny to remember the details of that moment. Steve, in his truck, was wearing one of those ghastly trucker hats and carrying a beer. And I had back my high heels and long fingernails, which had disappeared during our marriage. There is nothing significant about those little observations, except that I think they stood for the fact that, on some level, both Steve and I had had time to find ourselves again. The electricity was instant. I remembered exactly who it was that I had fallen head over heels in love with, and I know he remembered immediately what it was that had attracted him to me.

We drove up the coast, and Steve told me he was getting ready to move up to Santa Paula, with Barbara and the dozens of cars and trucks and motorcycles he had collected. Either he was speaking metaphorically or it was actually his plan. Either way, Steve was trying to tie up some loose ends in our emotional past.

I was thrown off by the power of the attraction I still felt for him, and I think it was mutual. But when he suggested that we pull off to the side of the highway near Oxnard and make love in an orange grove, I just couldn't do it. There was no way I could emotionally handle going from being the woman in his life to an occasional sexy interlude. I still cared far too much, and the proposition upset and saddened me.

After we visited his planes and his motorcycle collection and had a bite to eat in a little Santa Paula lunch place, we drove back. Something was still unfinished: the old relationship had been reopened. I was grateful for the fact that I was busy professionally and emotionally, because the possibility of getting involved with Steve at that point was more than I could deal with.

I never saw him again. Once, after a long silence, he called and asked to come over for supper, but it didn't work out. That Christmas, I tried to call Chad to send him my love. He was not at home, but I reached his best friend's mother. She told me that Steve had just been diagnosed with cancer at Cedars-Sinai Hospital.

I was in shock. I wrote Steve a very long letter, telling him how I felt about him and asking how I could help and what I could do for his two children. I put it in the hotel mail chute. While I was writing and crying I was drinking vodka, and the next morning I retrieved the letter, for fear of having said too much. I never mailed it.

In a few days the word was out: that he did not have cancer, that it was a false alarm. He made such a campaign of stopping the cancer rumor that most of us actually believed the good news. He hired a powerful press agent to deal with the gossip, and called his friends, including me, to tell us not to be concerned. But the lung X-ray that had been taken in the hospital had shown cancer, and someone had leaked that news to the press (as someone with no morality always does in those cases), and so the story persisted in spite of all Steve's hard work to the contrary.

Before long it was obvious to everyone that Steve was gravely ill, fighting for his life. Because of the way our marriage had ended I was never privy to firsthand information, and so I am unclear about the exact sequence of events. His cancer was diagnosed as having probably been caused by asbestos. Long before he became an actor, Steve had been exposed to it in the merchant marine, then in a tire factory in San Francisco, and again as a race car driver. His was a ravaging form of the disease.

He tried every modern means of beating it, but in the end he chose to fight his disease in a clinic in Mexico. He was closely guarded by his children and his first and last wives.

The last time I talked to Steve was when he called asking me to bring Josh up to Santa Paula to see him. He had assured me again that he was not ill, that he just missed Josh. Unfortunately, I could not drive Josh up there on the suggested day, and so we never did see him.

Looking back on events as I now know them, I think he was arranging that meeting so that he could see Josh again for the last time, and maybe me too.

There is nothing quite as upsetting as having big things left unsaid at the end of a relationship. And so much worse when the person dies and those important thoughts have not been expressed. I sent letters, but I have no way of knowing whether they ever reached him, in the piles of fan mail he received.

Once, while driving down the Pacific Coast Highway, I heard on the car radio a speech thanking the "wonderful people of Mexico" for helping with the fight against cancer. The voice was raspy, but I recognized it as Steve's. Evidently he was doing some kind of public relations favor for the controversial clinic and, at the same time, telling his fans around the world that he was grateful for their prayers and support. Hearing that strange voice made me pull the car over to the side of the road and cry.

People have often asked me why I did not go down to Mexico to visit Steve in the clinic. Certainly I wanted to. But my memory of him was of a man in perfect physical shape, and he preferred it to stay that way—at least that is what I was told. I also did not want to upset Barbara and Neile and the two children, who were all dealing with an unbearable amount of pain. I was sure there were at least a few sleazy photographers lurking around who would do anything to get a photograph of Ali MacGraw visiting Steve McQueen, and I knew Steve well enough to be sure that almost nothing would have upset him more than that kind of publicity. Any thought of my visiting that hospital struck me finally as totally selfish and inconsiderate. Because my notes and letters went unacknowledged, I could only hope that someone was conveying my concern and love.

It has taken years for me to sort out my pain about that unfinished business. What has finally worked for me has been my own deep faith that somehow we are all looped together in Infinity—that now, if not then, Steve knows that I love and forgive him. My strong personal conviction is that his tragic illness was fanned by a lifetime of anger and suspicion, and that rage and pain caused the fatal cancer.

How tragic it was that a man who had—or nearly

had—absolutely everything could have spent a lifetime feeling wary of his friends, vindictive toward his enemies, and certain that the whole world was out to do him in. I have ached for him, for the hugs and support he never had as a child. I am sorry for all the times that my own selfishness prevented me from looking beneath his thoughtlessness for the battered creature within. We met and fell in love at the wrong time in each of our lives. I am sure we are linked in some way together, forever.

On November 7, 1980, I got a phone call from his first wife, Neile. Steve was dead. Even in death they could not leave him alone. Some irresponsible photographer took a picture of him after death. I saw it on the cover of some New York paper and in *Paris Match*. I cannot believe that these photographers and editors and publishers don't have families and children of their own, when they make the disgusting decision to go ahead with their cheap photo journalism. It is so cruel.

A few weeks later Neile invited me to a small memorial at Steve's farm in Santa Paula, and told me if I would like to go, I could drive up with her and her husband. I was enormously touched by her thoughtfulness, as well as by her daughter Terry's.

Steve would have approved of the event. There was beer and potluck food, some close friends, and the comfort of a home that looked as though he had belonged and been happy there. Some of the guests were able to put aside grief and send him off in a rather celebratory mood. At the end of the afternoon several of his pilot buddies flew their antique planes over the little house in the formation of a crucifix, and it was all anyone could do to hold back the tears.

God bless you, Steve, wherever you are. I think of you nearly every day, and I hope you are healthy and free and that you know at last that you were loved and valued by many, many of us. You had the world by a golden string, and you will probably have it again. I hope you enjoy it next time. God bless you.

Interlude

I t is snowing furiously now—great white flakes twisting down in columns like strands of spun sugar in a pot of taffy. Sometimes the wind changes direction, driving the blizzard at a sharp angle into already white-coated tree trunks. Outside my window is one of the impossibly fat chickadees, doing his nails. Time has stood still for me here in this wonderful house in Maine. It is the gift I have been waiting for.

It is as though a big piece of my life had not yet happened. Or is it that I survived it? Every day I discover another book that was in my family's library, too: the big Leonardo da Vinci, my very edition of Thackeray's *Vanity Fair,* the Eugene Field *Poems of Childhood* with illustrations by Maxfield Parrish, *Madame Bovary,* the poems of Keats and Shakespeare and John Masefield, and my same two black volumes of Oscar Wilde. And every day a new discovery. As in my family's house, there is a collection of ancient, nearly pulverized children's books on the shelf near the floor behind my big chair. I wonder if they have *Rory O'Mory: The Fox That Chased the English Gentleman,* which Daddy illustrated shortly before I was born? I have the only copy of it I have ever seen, testament not only to the fact that Daddy did at least earn one paycheck in a lifetime, but that he was a gifted and underappreciated illustrator.

Am I just retreating to the comfort I had as a child, to familiar and stimulating memories? Or am I seeing things clearly? Both, I guess. Certainly this library, with familiar old books—the kind that smell good, in that musty, special way—is about people who have spent nearly half a century adding patch after small patch of information and literature and dreams to the whole, so that the final picture is never quite finished but continues to grow. Out where I live it seems to me that most people believe that if only they had enough money (and power) they could "arrive," be complete. I imagine that if you were in an airplane and looked down at us in Los Angeles you would discover that no one is really going anywhere—just round and round and round, under an ever-thickening smear of smog. From afar, here in blizzardy Maine, I see it as Ken and Barbie Land, down to the too-long curly hair and $400 cashmere cardigan on every groovy blue-jean-suited mini-agent on Rodeo Drive. I feel more myself here.

4

PLAYERS

In 1978 I made my first film since the break-up of my marriage to Steve. It was a harmless little summer movie called *Players,* about an "older woman," me, who falls in love with a handsome young tennis player (the late, charming Dean Paul Martin). From the beginning there were problems, but as we had been locked into filming the tennis sequences at Wimbledon that year, we had no choice but to proceed with the schedule. The producer was my ex-husband Robert Evans, and the director was Tony Harvey, who had been nominated for an Academy Award for *The Lion in Winter.*

That was the good part of this experience, and working with Tony marked the beginning of a lifelong friendship with a sensitive, talented man. Unfortunately, most of us thought the script could have used some more work, and the final film was not as good as it should have been.

One critic even called it "Bob Evans' revenge on Ali MacGraw." Nice.

I was sent to several European countries to promote *Players*. For a period of weeks, and in a variety of languages, interviewers would boil it down to "God, this film is awful. How come you did it?" It was as though I were standing on the bow of the *Titanic,* spotting the iceberg and saying, "Well, just aim for my heart."

The last part of this publicity tour took me to Germany.

The young interviewer sat in a chair at a big glass coffee table. I politely sat down across from him. "You know," I said, "we all start out to make the best movie we can, but sometimes it disappoints you."

He interrupted to bring in a girl who was all done up in her version of "cool" American: black leather, fishnet stockings and micro-mini. She was not introduced to me, but she joined us at the coffee table. I was quietly seething because I was sure he had said to her: "Hey—you want to come upstairs with me and have a look at Ali MacGraw? I'm interviewing her."

He said to me in his German accent, "Um . . . why do you get a million dollars for a movie? How do you justify that?"

I made a joke out of it because I had never earned anywhere near that amount of money in my life. "God, I must call my accountant," I said, "because I'm missing hundreds and hundreds and hundreds of thousands of dollars."

But he continued. "I mean, how do you justify getting so much money?"

I leaped horizontally across the table and I grabbed

him by the throat and said, my face right in his face, "BECAUSE I DESERVE IT."

There was a split-second pause, and then he said, inching his chair imperceptibly closer, "Well, you know, I'm really not all that interested in movies. What I really like is rock 'n' roll. I know that you go out with musicians and know everybody.

"I'm coming to the Coast," he continued. "Can I call you? Because I'd like to meet a lot of musicians."

Just Tell Me What You Want was made the year after *Players*. It is my most recent feature film, and although few saw it at the theaters, it has become something of a video classic.

I nearly did not do the film. Sue Mengers told me she had been lucky enough to get me a meeting with Sidney Lumet to see about playing the female lead in the film version of Jay Presson Allen's novel about a rich, spoiled, powerful man and the rich, spoiled woman who was his mistress. I said, rather high-handedly, that I had not loved the novel, and that, as the studio was not particularly thrilled to use me, what was the point of going on a wild goose chase to New York?

To my amazement, I got the part of Bones, playing opposite Alan King, with a cast that included Myrna Loy and Keenan Wynn and Dina Merrill and Peter Weller. I was so well supported by all this talent and by Jay's terrific script that the movie turned out to be one of which I am very proud and which brought some good reviews. Sidney is the consummate actor's director, and he coaxed a real performance out of me. There were three full weeks of rehearsals, to which we were told to come with the entire script memorized. This is an unusual luxury in films, where, more often than not, the actors arrive on the set with just a few days of rehearsal time before the panic of filming. Sidney's way of working gives the actor a chance to stretch out and explore, and therefore give a richer performance, because by the time the actual shooting begins, many of the mistakes and most of the fear are gone.

It was Christmastime in New York, and I have a hilarious memory of learning the script in between making Christmas cookies and wrapping presents. My mother, recently widowed, was with us for the holidays, and she offered to hear my lines every night the way she had helped me memorize poetry at Rosemary Hall so many years before. It was a sweet, comforting offer. After dinner I would study my thousands of lines of tough, smart-ass dialogue, so that Mummy could review them with me in the quiet of early morning. I shall never forget my conservative elderly mother correcting me: I said, "Fuck you, asshole—that's a lot of shit."

"No, dear, it's 'You shit-ass, go fuck yourself.'" She never cracked a smile. Page after page.

I arrived at the first rehearsal with my dialogue memorized as well as anyone's and experienced the thrill of working with plenty of time on a finished script with a brilliant director and cast, and no insanity.

The preparation paid off. *Just Tell Me What You Want* is a film, like *Goodbye, Columbus,* that I can look at without cringing. I learned a great deal about acting from Sidney and was proud of myself. Together with all involved, we created fine entertainment. There were no sloppy accidents, and in fact, we rehearsed the famous fight scene, like a dance sequence. The floor of the rehearsal studio was marked off with different colors of masking tape to indicate the various steps, so that the cinematographer and Sidney could perfectly plot the camera moves before we actually showed up on the real set. As a result, the day of the real fight went as smoothly as one/two/three/ kick poor Alan King/four/five/six/bash him with my handbag/seven/eight/nine/smother him with my huge fisher coat . . . and so on until the whole ground floor of Bergdorf Goodman was demolished.

On the Sunday morning when we filmed this destruction of Bergdorf's, I invited my mother to walk over to the store to watch us shoot. It was the first time in my nearly ten-year career that she had ever seen me work. At the end of the morning, with Alan King's nose pouring blood from one of my attacks, and my hair dripping sweat from the workout, my mother looked at us all in a kind of wonder and amazement. "My goodness, dear. I had no idea you worked so hard!"

After all those years of thinly veiled disapproval, Mummy had finally almost paid me a compliment.

A spring day in 1982: I was in Yugoslavia, where I had spent most of the year making the epic miniseries *The Winds of War*.

I made a two-day excursion during a break in the filming to go with two new actor friends and my young driver Mitya into the country.

On either side of our speeding car were fields of brilliant yellow buttercups and fat red clovers and dandelions turned to halos of fluff. The grass and new leaves were just-born green, and the air smelled the way I remember May smelling when I was a child. The closest sight and smell I could match it to in Malibu were those fields of mustard and mauve grass where Steve and I used to sit. I missed him. I missed what he meant to me: the safety from everything I might ever fear. I was haunted by him each day.

We drove through village after village, each with red brick houses and at least one church. The architecture is faintly Byzantine—onionlike domes underneath a cross, and arched windows trimmed in white. I missed my mother, who had died almost two years before. She would have adored this trip.

Mitya took us to a restaurant in the hill town of Momjan, surrounded by wild flowers and tall silky grass. Here, the thickets of acacia trees are overwhelming with their perfume. The restaurant was funny and very loud—students singing raucously at varnished pine tables laden with beer and wine and light deep-fried dough covered with powdered sugar. We ate huge steaks and salads, chasing them with the local grappa and homemade wine served to us in jugs shaped like cream pitchers. Back at our hotel we had a novel and extremely lethal after-dinner drink called a Nicolashka: a belt of vignac, deceptively sweet and mild, then a slice of lemon covered in finely ground coffee and sugar, which you eat and chase with more vignac. The assault on the stomach is just amazing, not to mention the ensuing hangover.

On the second day we drove a dazzling route through vineyards and terra-cotta earth. The roadside was strewn with poppies and bluebonnet and mustard; old, old stone farmhouses with perfect gardens; and then miles of scallions and potatoes. We stopped at the ancient town of Porec—cobbled streets and a busy, seaside feeling—where we had huge ice-cream cones served to us by a theatrical fellow who threw the scoops across the room; one error landed on a lady's face.

The country changes so dramatically there that in an hour we were in twisting hill country, filled with miniature towns, always immaculate. Each one is slightly different—very symmetrical, a little Eastern, and always there is a basilica. We drove to an old mountain town called Motovun, with skinny streets and a 360-degree view into infinity. The village is walled, and the coat of arms of Venice hangs over each entrance arch. The memory I have now is of little patios and gardens and cats and murmurs all around us—silent, secret summer places. Then three and a half hours to Lake Bled.

It was as though we had seen three different countries that day: coast, mountain, and lake. Bled is a perfect Alpine village of storybook houses set amid snowcapped mountains and overlooking a lake. There is a castle on the hillside and one little hotel after another along the water, where iridescent green-headed mallards, speckled brown geese, and swans with their young swim among lotus blossoms. There are huge candelabra chestnuts and dozens of wild flowers along the shore, and everywhere people walking quietly, or just sitting by the lake. People here seemed to be older, and I thought again that Mummy and Daddy would have adored the day's drive and, most especially, Lake Bled.

Finally, we drove to the brilliant green valley where Mitya was raised. We met his grandparents and his mother. No one was expecting him, and it was very moving to see these people together. We all felt that he had planned the trip to unfold in an increasingly intimate fashion, with the final treat being a long mountain walk to the cascades he played in as a child.

.   .   .

ONE OF MY great memories of filming *The Winds of War* will always be the scene in which the Jewish refugees cross Poland, hauling all their belongings with them. The art and prop departments had outdone themselves. As far as the eye could see the line stretched out, so real to me that I felt I was part of the actual historical event. There was a black-and-white hearse, ornate like an ice-cream wagon. There were dozens of dignified old women, dressed head to toe in black, their faces inscrutable and long-suffering. There were farm horses weighted down with pots and pans and bundles of clothing, and there were awkward foals who followed their mothers. There were young men and grandfathers, pregnant women and frightened young children and family dogs, and a few people on bicycles. It was easy to imagine a whole nation fleeing the Nazis, an endless line of innocents against an infinity of wild-flower-speckled farmland.

And everywhere there was the anachronism of rain-coated movie people rushing in and out of these lines, holding their soggy breakfast sandwiches and coffee, and acting as though this were a perfectly normal way to behave on a rainy May day.

Next we filmed the wedding in Medize. The wardrobe and makeup departments were up at 4:30 to prepare the entire cast of the Warsaw Theater, who had been hired to play Hassidic Jews in this very orthodox ceremony. The wedding was staged in a huge, arched concrete barn, dressed to look like a moonlit courtyard. There were tall branches of spring leaves banked everywhere to look like trees, from which hung oil lamps, twinkling in the movie-made moonlight. It was magical. The Hassidic elders wore, beside their *payes*, large black hats and long skinny black satin overcoats over black trousers, white collarless shirts, and a cloth of black and white. The coat is tied with a very long grosgrain ribbon to separate the upper from the lower half of the body. They were all elegant, and the most intriguing of all was a handsome young man who stood a head taller than the rest. I had a little crush on him. He turned out to be a criminologist from Montenegro and didn't speak a word of any language I knew.

Later came the scene of wild and ecstatic dancing, the men together on one side, the women holding handkerchiefs and whirling in pinwheels with each other on the opposite side, and finally everyone together in a frenzy of fiddle music. It was a fifteen-hour workday, but imagine being paid for that work; to me, it felt like being at a party.

I felt proud to be part of this film. I thought it was going to be a masterpiece.

WHEN *The Winds of War* appeared on television as a much heralded and hyped miniseries, it made the cover of *Time*. In the issue of February 7, 1983, Gerald Clarke wrote: "The only really bad performance, in fact, is MacGraw's." I was stunned. I, who am usually overly critical of everything I do, still could not believe that I had been singled out as the worst part of this project.

The normal clues to my alcoholism were not incoherence and drunken behavior, but in my shock and devastation at this review and others, I put in a solid week of blackout drinking.

Looking back on it, the *Dynasty* experience was bizarre from the very beginning. Once again Sue Mengers, who had correctly cajoled me into reading for *Just Tell Me What You Want*, suggested that I do thirteen episodes of the blockbuster nighttime soap opera. "Better take it, honey, because the money and exposure are extraordinary, and you might never have another job."

I believed her. I had never watched the show, but I knew that it was the most popular program on television, starring a number of beautiful women with perfect bodies and hairdos that never moved. One viewing of it convinced me that I did not qualify, but the financial offer was indeed staggering, and my huge ego responded to the notion that this would be a very Big Pop Comeback after the personal debacle of *The Winds of War*.

And so I showed up for work, concerned that I had

neither the looks nor the expertise to pull off this weird art form, nighttime soap opera. How right I was.

From the first day, when, from behind a huge and beautiful arrangement of flowers, the leading man welcomed me to the set, I knew I was in for some serious problems—such as, how do I say these words? Why can't I just toss them off with style and a bit of a wicked send-up, like Joan Collins?

One day, early on, I was dithering around in some chrome-yellow designer suit, playing with a tea set and wondering how in God's name I was going to be able to say my dialogue, when the time came for my close-up. The business of the day had something to do with Big Money from the Orient, and I guess I must have been part of a summit meeting—who could ever figure it out logically? Anyway, just as I had decided that no one could ever deliver with a straight face the lines I had been given, I heard John Forsythe speak his line to a group of Japanese extras: "Size isn't everything, Mr. Wang." He never even cracked a smile, although the crew was on the floor. I was in big trouble.

I had been hired to seduce America's sweetheart, Blake Carrington, played by John Forsythe, at the same time that Rock Hudson had been hired to seduce America's other sweetheart, Krystle (Linda Evans). Fans were evidently quivering with the imagined scenes: the scandal in Denver, the making-up, the tears, the dresses, the hairdos! There was just one little problem: John didn't believe that America wanted Blake and his virtuous wife, Krystle (*Krystle,* as in pure!), to behave as trashily as the other members of the blockbuster show, and so every time my character, Lady Ashley, leaned toward Blake to kiss him, he would pull to the side and mutter something about "Krystle, Krystle. . . ." Finally, when it was clear that, plot line or not, the leading man was not going to sleep with this particularly aggressive woman, the writers decided to rescript and sic me on the handsome young lead, actor John James, whose great love, Fallon, had somehow disappeared when the plot had taken a twist to accommodate the actress's exit from the show. Once again, excitement mounted in the TV dream factory. But alas, he, too, turned his cheek and muttered the name of his lost love. By now I had put in some ten weeks as a rejected woman on prime time.

Also, the corporate powers had come to hate my un-teased hair and wooden acting. America was writing let-ters to ABC begging them to dump Lady Ashley. One day as Lady Ashley and her new young lover were hav-ing a coy little breakfast, he glanced at a newspaper between bites of croissant and suddenly spied the face of his dear departed wife, Fallon. His eyesight was re-markable. The black-and-white photo, taken at a soccer stadium, showed at least 200,000 spectators. If the script-writer had rediscovered Fallon, I knew that my days were numbered. I would be eliminated in the great end-of-the-season holocaust, the details of which were so secret that even the actors were not given the script.

Sensing doom, I asked Nolan Miller, the gentle and elegant costume designer, to give Lady Ashley a huge cabbage rose in her hat, right above the eye. When the guerrilla terrorists came swinging through the candy-glass windows of the set that day, looking like so many orangutans at a church social, a "bullet" caught me in the rose, and I fell to the floor like the rest of the cast. I did not know whether I was meant to close my eyes and lie still, or stare like a Keane painting at the ceiling. Between takes I asked the associate producer, who, in a rapture of theatrical pleasure, had grabbed a plastic bottle of false blood from the makeup man and was squirting it all over us. "Closed, stupid," she said. "You're dead."

And that was how, in front of three hundred extras, I learned that my services would no longer be needed on *Dynasty*. I felt terrible, but I almost laughed when the same woman asked me if I would give her some tips on how to decorate her house—free.

Just about everyone in the world managed to see at least one episode of Lady Ashley's brief run on *Dynasty*, so the experience was good for a year of supermarket fodder—both on the printed page and in person. Once, when I was going through the checkout line in Trancas, a particularly hostile woman whom I had seen regularly over the years at PTA meetings and soccer matches, glared at me and snapped, "How *could* you do that to darling Krystle?" I knew I had somehow arrived.

IN HINDSIGHT I can see that I was not trained to do the style of acting required on a show like *Dynasty*. That is a skill unto itself, and only a few actors seem able to pull it off with any credibility, week after week. To be perfectly honest, I was scarcely trained at all as an actress, and the moment had arrived when I could no longer get by on energy and personality.

It was a scary realization, a long time coming. With the end of *Dynasty* and no attendant fanfare or job offers, I came up against the reality that my career was in serious trouble, that there were no flashy moves left with which to put it back on track. I think my fears and embarrassment were heightened by the fact that my whole career in Hollywood had been subject to inordinate hype from the very beginning. With three back-to-back blockbuster movies as a start, I was completely unprepared for the lean times, and the pressure gnawed at me twenty-four hours a day. It puzzles me, today, that I did not take advantage of the moment to go to school and really study acting; it might have been the logical way to deal with the feelings I was starting to have, of being utterly without talent.

From the beginning, though, I had always thought that one of the great rewards of working as a film actress was the long stretches of time between jobs. Because my bills were paid by working for relatively few months of the year, this meant that I had more of what I called "real life" time.

When *Dynasty* ended, I guess I told myself that the lull was just another in a career of similar pauses. It never occurred to me that, with the exception of a dreadful little film I did for English television, I was in for a stretch of unemployment that would go on for years. I was constantly busy, as I always have been, with activities ranging from the routine of being the parent of a young boy to all kinds of work with different charity organizations. And as long as I didn't allow myself to peek beneath the superficial explanations of why I was no longer being offered film or television roles, I was reasonably happy.

When I was growing up, I really did absorb all those lessons from my mother: that we have a responsibility to give something back to our society, that a healthy and sane planet does not just "happen." She taught me to give not only money but time to causes which particularly touch me. As there is never enough time or money to make more than a microscopic dent in the world's pain, I had to choose areas which, for various reasons, affected me the most intensely. They include the rights of children and animals, the environment, and the community in which Josh and I lived—in this case, Malibu, where I served as honorary mayor for two years. At times I became involved in various tragic situations all over the world. When I look back on my daily calendar of those out-of-work post-*Dynasty* years, I see that the amount of time I spent on a wide variety of these causes probably prevented me from feeling like a total failure as a human being. Those meetings and phone calls and rallies often kept me too busy to scrutinize what had happened to my career.

In addition, there were still enough discussions about half-baked projects for me to delude myself that I was still "working"; there was the rigorous workout regimen I have always maintained; and there were many wonderful hours spent with my friends, and traveling.

Ever since I started to work in the film business I have treated location work as an opportunity to share exotic trips with Joshua. By the time he was fourteen he had visited not only most of Europe, but Asia and Kenya as well. These were fabulous adventures for us, and on each one I insisted that he keep his own journal; usually his teachers required that he do that anyway, in lieu of homework. Between the two of us we have a rich collection of souvenirs. In 1982, I was lucky to be invited to do a documentary on endangered species in Africa; the next year I did a television film in Hong Kong, and we spent Joshua's spring vacation afterward in Beijing. We celebrated my birthday, that cold and windy April Fool's Day, on the Great Wall of China; we were with a new friend from Hong Kong, and for some reason we seemed to be almost the only people at the Wall that day. We imagined that someone could have spotted us from the moon, where, we were told, the only man-made monument visible is that serpentine wall. Another time I was invited to be a judge at the Tokyo Music Festival, and I took Joshua with me to experience Japan. And during one extraordinary decorating job, we were invited to spend the summer on a boat in the Mediterranean. It all added up to a lot of very exciting time, with or without starring roles in films. And I floated along, grateful for the chance to enjoy these experiences with my son.

In addition to our time together traveling, I did what most mothers I know do: I stayed involved in my son's activities, in and out of school. There was always something very reassuring to me about the day-to-day minutiae of soccer games and school projects, parent meetings and birthday parties. I devoted a lot of time to these everyday involvements, grateful for the opportunity to be an active part of my son's childhood and development. Because we lived in a very family-oriented community, and because we participated a lot in the various activities in Malibu, Josh had a much more "normal" upbringing than he might have, given the parents and stepparents he had. I am thankful for those periods of sweet sanity, because they will probably be important to Josh in the years to come.

As for me, I realize now that rich as those years were,

I was also working overtime to avoid examining my career. I was busy running in too many different directions to analyze the reality that I was not only beginning to drink too much, but I was acting out some pretty dysfunctional behavior with men. My disappointment and even shame at feeling like a public failure, in a career for which I had been celebrated, only added to my secret fear that, finally, "they" had discovered I was a fraud.

For a long time I convinced myself that I was a very free spirit when it came to my relationships with men. I concocted some kind of warped feminist jargon to tell myself that I was not only open and available, but also admirably straightforward. The truth is, for decades I was incapable of any real intimacy except for sex. Most of the rest of my behavior was pretty controlled, including my so-called honesty. I was totally out of touch with who I was, yet I fooled myself into thinking I was refreshingly uninhibited. Lots of times, I was, if not flat-out drunk, at least thoroughly buzzed, because, I guess, I was a lot more frightened than I realized. And if I was not high on alcohol, I was certainly high on my favorite concoction, Romance.

Romance, for me, was usually just heat. There was one relationship I entered into because I knew I wanted to be taken care of, and there were others I fell into because I guess that on some subconscious level I wanted to explore different facets of my own personality. More than once, I know I got into a relationship to test just how crazy I could get.

There was a lot of very sophisticated sexual behavior in the seventies. More than one man in my life has suggested that it would be much more fun if the evening could include some wide-eyed, voluptuous bimbo he knew. I interpreted this need as reflecting gross inadequacy on my part; maybe I didn't "do it" well. One night, when I was no longer married, I had a pretty wild party in my as-yet-unfurnished little beach house. There was lots of food, lots of tequila, and enough cocaine to keep everyone going all night. One couple had made it pretty obvious that the evening could continue long after the party ended, if I wanted. Well, I liked them, and I thought, "Why not?" I was curious to find out whether this was something that thrilled *me*, never mind the men who always suggested it.

The funny thing is, the experience resulted in rug burns on all our backs, from the newly installed sisal carpeting. And I spent most of my time trying not to hurt the girl's feelings by being too attracted to her husband. When the evening was over, at dawn, I realized once and for all, and without judgment or guilt, that there are other ways of spending my bedtime that I like better. It had nothing to do with inadequacy: just apples and oranges, as they say.

I HAVE been married three times, and in between those marriages I lived with several men in relationships that were monogamous. Amazingly enough, I was able to tell my parents the truth about where and how I was living without their ever uttering .a murmur about my life style—until each episode was over. Then they would regale me with the details of their disapproval and relief. I appreciated their restraint, which was unusual for parents in that era.

Since my divorce from Steve, I have not actually *lived* with any man, and I have had long, healthy periods of no involvement whatever. In looking back over the choices I have made these past dozen years, I have to admit that more often enough than not, I have moved from crush to love affair at 200 miles an hour, without ever doing the real homework on who this new man was.

So I am afraid there are more than a few men whom I virtually invented to suit my needs and dreams of the moment. When am I going to learn?

I WILL call him Jamie.

Jamie knocked my socks off, took my breath away. He was a poet, a professor, a drug addict, a ladies' man, and a liberal. He was ravishingly handsome, famously married, and, with the whisper of the words "I love you," my candidate for Mr. Right. From the instant I laid eyes on him I was done for. I was having a tough time in my then marriage, and I longed to hear the words "I've waited all my life for you." I heard them, and I believed them. I had to. I was married; he was married; we were both stoned. And so began the nightmare obsession of my grown-up life—a year of crazed behavior, with me starring in a real-life edition of *Fatal Attraction*.

I learned something important. "I love you" doesn't necessarily mean that. Sometimes it just means "I want to sleep with you." And sometimes that does not include any dusting-off time later. Eat and run.

But Jamie was my fatal attraction, and I closed my ears to everything that did not fit into my fantasy of going off into the sunset together. Jamie was a brooding loner, afraid and suspicious of everyone but passionate about his politics, which were honorable and outspoken. He had no interest whatever in company or food or travel or play. He materialized from the little room in which he wrote only when summoned.

He wrote me a poem, called "High and Easy," and read it out loud in front of a lot of people we hardly knew. I didn't get it. I told him it was great.

He would come into my life for a quick spin of my heart, and then look at me with the closest approximation to loathing that I have ever seen in a man. He gave me plenty of time to heal without him, and then he would reappear, all his charms intact. And once more I was done for.

On the memorable final night, he phoned me at three-thirty in the morning to tell me: "So long, kid. It's been great." The next morning he was on a plane for Europe to join his wife. I wrote and rewrote a letter explaining how Perfect I was for him, how much we Belonged Together, how Devastating this all was. Thank God I never gave him that letter. It was all humiliating enough.

For months I turned up at all his lectures and book-signings. At each of them there would be another beautiful woman (not his wife), anointed, as I had been, for the moment. He looked at me as though he had never seen me before in his life, and I died. This went on for at least a year—forever, it seemed. I just did not get it. I wanted it to turn out my way. It never did. It's just as well.

MICKEY RAPHAEL and I have not been together (as they say) for at least six years, but we have remained close. In a funny way, I trust him more than any man I have ever known. He has no guile, no hidden agenda whatsoever. He is present in every way, and has a drop-dead sense of humor that is never at anyone's expense. He has no cutting edge, no competitiveness, and yet is probably the best there is at what he does. Mickey plays harmonica with Willie Nelson's band.

I fell for Mickey the first time I saw him play. We met, and shortly after that we started to see each other. Then I went off to Yugoslavia and Italy for *The Winds of War*. All the while I was there we talked daily on the phone. That turns out to be what musicians do on the road.

Mickey had none of the insane trappings of many of his peers. I was safe, and I knew it. Back in the States, I loved going to the concerts. I loved the way all the people involved with Willie welcomed me, once they decided I was all right. I felt I belonged. I don't know that I have ever felt more secure in a social situation. Whatever it was that they all liked about me, I felt it had to do with my real self.

The truth is, I also loved the times in between, when we did not see each other, because I was also wrapped up in the details of being a suburban mother to an adolescent. The rhythm was terrific.

For some reason I slowly began to feel that I was too old and maybe even too "experienced" to stay in the relationship, and one day we sort of drifted apart. I worried that Mickey might wake up one morning having changed his mind about me and there I would be, sixty years old or something.

All I wish for Mickey is that he have every single dream imaginable come true, and that his friendship and affection and loyalty will be there for me to count on forever.

I DON'T know anything at all about football; I do not understand it—in fact, I hate it. About the only thing I enjoy about football is some of the great bodies of the players, none of whose teams I can ever remember. I don't even try. Even when I went to college I was the only person who did not know who was playing whom every Saturday. Poor Josh. When he was younger he was a fanatic sports fan. He knew the name of every single player in every single sport. He assumed that his mother was a half-wit in that department.

And my own athletic ability has always been pretty pathetic. Once, when I was about ten, I kicked a mean and altogether surprising goal in an otherwise all-boys' soccer match in elementary school. I was a hero for a day, but it wasn't a feat I would repeat in the years to come, not in tennis or girls' basketball or field hockey or softball.

But my first serious boyfriend in college was a football player—the captain, in fact, of the Haverford College team and a fellow waiter in the summer at Haddon Hall in Atlantic City. I loved being the girlfriend of a football star. It somehow legitimized me.

And once, some years ago, I had a huge crush on a world-class quarterback. He was introduced to me by a mutual friend, and the proverbial sparks flew from the first moment. He was bright and funny and sexy and rich, and about the easiest company I've ever met. We carried on one of those furtive arrangements that happen when one of you (it was me) is already officially "involved" with someone else. I remember, that Christmas, sitting all alone in my living room, staring hypnotized at the lights on the tree and wondering why I wasn't with him in Hawaii. We talked for hours by phone, two people who hardly knew each other—I by my Christmas tree, and he all tan and easy by the golf course, cool drink in hand.

It was mostly a phone romance—phone flirt would be a better word—but great fun and pretty hot. Once in a while we would manage a dinner or a drive out to some obscure part of Los Angeles, but mostly this liaison existed in my fantasy.

One day he looked at me and told me very nicely and firmly that I was "just too goddamned independent." And that was that. We parted friends, and he went on to be more and more successful.

I still don't know anything about football, although I picked up a few words along the way. Josh wanted me to remember the words *Pittsburgh Steelers,* and for his tenth birthday I made a cake with hundreds of brown and yellow M & M's in honor of his loyalty and passion for those guys.

Another phrase I picked up was *half time*. Half time:

a break in a long, hard game when the crowd gets to watch some high-stepping diversion, and the players have time to wipe off the sweat, bandage some wounds, and take a few minutes to figure out how to do it right the next half.

And that is where I am, at half time. Like the players, I've put some medicine on my wounds; like the crowd, I am listening to some snappy music. I'm no football player, but I am ready to play the second half. Hard and fun.

In 1985, I accepted a request to join the cast of a TV special called *Night of 100 Stars,* which actually turned out to be "Night of Something Like 340 Stars"— night*mare,* for short. I was so needy of recognition I would have done anything to prove to my out-of-work self that I was still, in fact, a "star."

This television show was such a gigantic production that if you blinked, reaching for your popcorn, you might have missed such legends as Sir Laurence Olivier, Danny Kaye, and half the Olympic team. For about sixteen hours we all waited around Radio City Music Hall for our chance to walk across that huge stage: several minutes each for the Big Stars (who worked mainly for the host network, ABC) and less than sixty seconds for those of us on our way Down.

At the end of this spectacle—after it had been taped,

stop-and-start style, for hours and hours—we crossed a strip of red carpet from the stage entrance to the Hilton Hotel to sit down for dinner with the fans who had paid up to $1,000 each to see their favorites. Except for the scant minute actually spent walking across the Radio City stage, most of my sixteen hours were spent in the Rockettes' dressing room. There, for hour upon hour, I watched transfixed as the Really Big Television Stars painted their eyelids with sparkly blue eye shadow and worked dark blush-on into their new breasts to increase the cleavage.

When the spectacle was over, I realized how very small a star I had become. My ego was battered, and when I arrived at the dreaded dinner at around two o'clock in the morning, I was grateful to be sitting with friends. Someone had craftily removed the big number from our centerpiece, so that none of the fans scheduled to sit at our table would ever find it. We had an exhausted, giddy dinner, and laughed and carried on and drank champagne—my first glass (then bottle) in the thirty days since I had vowed to my son that I would not drink anymore.

That night I wound up drunk, with an unexpected albeit very attractive guest in bed, and the next morning I had a hangover that lasted the entire flight home.

It was just one illustration of the disease I was carrying, and about to become aware of.

5

FADE-OUT

In the mid-eighties I got myself entangled in what I pray will be the last adulterous relationship of my life—this time with a sweet and very powerful entertainment executive, "Ben," who was married. We fell in love, and the ensuing months were filled with secrecy and urgency and the feelings of dishonesty and shame that are the fodder of all adultery. Finally, it is not for me. In the end no one wins—not the man, not the woman, and not the other woman or man.

The marriage broke up, though I never assumed it was because of me. And I, in my old make-believe world, assumed that we would share some kind of crescendo of togetherness. But it did not happen that way; to the contrary, he became more and more embroiled in his very demanding job. As our time together became increasingly compromised by the needs of his business, I became sadder and more difficult to be with. Seeing myself as a has-been in a business in which I had once been the Flavor of the Month just added to my envy and sullenness. I was certainly no treat to be with, particularly if the evening centered around entertaining the ambitious wife of a superstar, or when the early dawn was shattered by a business call that I wished could wait until office hours.

One Sunday morning, very, very early, the phone rang in our bedroom with the message that some associate was being transferred to the London office. It was a disheartening way to wake up on a Sunday morning, and I summoned all my anger to announce that I could no longer take third, fourth—even twelfth place to the Hollywood Hotline.

FOR TEN days I wept, managing to climb out of bed only to get Josh off to school and to go to my exercise class, where I tried to exhaust myself physically and wear down some of my rage. Every day in class, as I strained to touch my hands to my toes in a pretzel contortion, tears sprang to my eyes and I hurriedly left to go home and pull the covers over my head. I thought I was sobbing for a shattered love affair, but in reality I was sobbing because once more I had invented a person and a relationship, and awakened to find that the reality had nothing to do with my wishful thinking.

In a subtle and nasty way I made Ben question the value of what he was doing, of how he was spending his time. What right did I have to do that? He was always loving and generous and supportive of me. It was simply that we had very different life dreams, and the longer we were together, the more apparent it became.

As the days wore by and I was spending more and more of my time in bed with the covers pulled over my head to block out the pain, I grew frightened I was having a nervous breakdown. I envisioned a mental hospital, Thorazine—heavy sedation from the famous men in white coats.

One day my neighbor Lynda came by to see if I was feeling any better. Casually she left me a copy of a book on alcoholism—why, I had no idea. Since leaving Ben I had not dared to drink even a glass of wine for fear that I would drown myself in the ocean, or plow my car into a tree. I looked through the book very casually, thinking it was certainly not wonderful literature. If I wanted to deal with depression, I would prefer to read some good poetry.

At one point I flipped through the book and came across a sentence that talked about admitting we were alcoholic, that our lives had become unmanageable. I couldn't see that the first phrase applied to me, but the second half sure did. My life was, for the first time I could remember, totally out of control, and I was scared.

Lynda and another friend, Jeff Wald, who had recently recovered from massive cocaine addiction, suggested I go to a detox center to investigate what was going on. It seemed like an interesting, if not the only, solution. I thought about it, even made some preliminary investigations, but then another friend suggested that I just had a "broken heart" and that I deserved several weeks of pampering at the Golden Door. That sounded good. Another friend offered me her cabin in the solitude of Montana, where I might write and sketch, and heal my broken heart. And my ex-husband Bob generously and caringly offered to send me and Josh to the South of France for the summer, to get away from my routine life in Malibu.

It all sounded tempting, but a little voice in me said that all those alternatives were just soothing bandages, and that the real problem could only be solved by jumping smack into my own rubbish pail and dealing with the massive pile of garbage with which I had smothered my life.

I was thoroughly frightened at the condition my life was in, and I guess that—as usual—I hoped it would all "just go away." After several weeks of weighing the other offers and possibilities, however, I decided that I would at least try a detox facility. More in resignation than in any kind of certainty that I belonged there, I picked up the phone and called the Betty Ford Center. I arranged to be registered under a false name, so that the big computer at the hospital could not betray my privacy. I figured it was up to me to decide when and whether I wanted to tell anyone where I was going to be in July 1986.

The woman in Admissions came up with a great name: Lani Wolff! I envisioned a back-combed bimbo with porcelain nails from the San Fernando Valley, maybe a beautician—anyone but Ali MacGraw, movie star. Privacy assured, I was driven to Palm Springs by Lynda. As we passed the Hadley Date Shake stand in the Mojave, I wanted to leap out of the car and take the waiting Greyhound bus to wherever it was going. The whole Palm Springs area made me uneasy. I had spent a lot of time there in the early stages of my marriage to Steve, and while some of those memories were wonderful and loving and sexy, some were not. Some were even pretty tense, like the time Steve and I had one of our epic fights and I chartered a plane so that I could be hundreds of miles away when he returned from his motorcycle ride.

The Betty Ford Center is a perfectly simple little collection of mocha and cream stucco buildings, not so very different from a Holiday Inn in its affection for orange and ocher decor. "Spare" is a voluptuous description of the rooms.

And there, in a small, shared bedroom, I embarked upon my most terrifying and life-changing experience.

THEY TOLD us we would have chores to do, like setting the tables, vacuuming the hallways, announcing the various mandatory activities. I liked the sound of that. No frills. Just work. Do your own laundry. Go to every single meeting and group encounter and meal. Absolutely no free private time in which to isolate and brood. I was ready. I had packed some old wash-and-wear clothes, and I brought almost nothing else except for a good-luck necklace of tribal amulets that my friend Jewels had made me and a pair of cross-shaped crystal earrings—I figured I needed all the luck I could get. This was going to be thirty days of brutal work. I checked in knowing I had made the right choice, but still stuck in what they call "denial." "I do not really think I'm an alcoholic," I primly told the staff. "I'm just terribly sad, and my life has become unmanageable." I did my best acting to portray a genteel lady with a severely broken heart—a little mixed up, perhaps, but basically just in need of a tune-up.

It took me a little over twenty-four hours to understand that what I needed was not a little tune-up but, rather, major collision work, new parts for everything. I felt oddly relieved that I was not literally crazy, that there was an acceptable label for what was wrong with me, and a highly successful program for taking the pain and shame and violent mood swings out of my life.

I rather quickly got it that this program was going to deal, in the most painful detail, with *how* I felt, and not—as in past experiences in analysis—with the reasons *why*. During my marriage to Steve, I had spent hours and hours as well as thousands of dollars in therapy with a man who listened to me rant and occasionally cry about my childhood. But since he never commented on anything, I don't know whether he slept through, or reeled at, my tales of life with Steve McQueen. Probably he helped me muster the courage to leave that marriage, but never once did he ask me whether or not I drank—and if so, how much. Sooner or later I would have to have admitted that I could almost never have just one drink, and that I couldn't think of a single social situation that I dared to go into without first having "just a little something." This kind of behavior is now part of the general consciousness of alcoholism, but back then it was a very rare therapist who got into the question of addiction and the feelings that it cauterizes.

I did spend ten sessions with one woman whose methods were unorthodox for the time. But in retrospect, her imaging and conversations were not unlike the work that is done at the treatment center, and I am grateful for at least that taste of a more interactive therapy. My own mind has worked overtime, all my life, as I have tried to analyze and understand everything, and I know that this has distanced me even more from my emotions. As I hammered away at the minute details of my childhood, I needed to learn that my parents—like most—were perfectly decent people doing the very best they could in difficult circumstances, and screwing up. Just like us. I prefer the idea that we actually have some present-day responsibility for how we want to live, rather than that we are prisoners of our upbringing.

In the months to come I would realize beyond a doubt that my whole angry, self-righteous diatribe about my latest relationship with Ben was rubbish, that I had been as selfish and controlling and judgmental and hurtful as I had labeled him. Now, years later, when I read my journal, I marvel at my ignorance in the ranting I did at this man.

I learned huge lessons in my month in treatment. My journal, required nightly, indicates how much I began to grow.

Day 1 — I have never felt more lonely and scared in my life. My stomach is in knots. Some of it is from almost no sleep last night, but mostly it is due to the terror, loneliness, and shock I feel realizing that I have checked myself into a center for chemical abuse. No more hiding behind my bullshit of the "sometime alcoholic."

I am on the verge of crying, as I have been for at least four months now. Correction: I have been sobbing every several hours, daily, for the past four months as I watched my fourteen-month-old love affair unravel. I made an impossible choice when I fell into an obsessive, "romantic" passion with Ben. Perhaps I even invented him, paying no attention to all the signals that we were on two different paths. I have done that before, God knows, and once again the end of the affair has reduced me to a feeling of total invalidation.

I am here at the Center because I began to scare myself with the intensity of my feelings of worthlessness and unattractiveness—the certainty that I was not and would never be worth loving.

I am very clearly blocked. I know that alcohol (and drugs) make it impossible for any spiritual healing to take place, and yet I have often had much more to drink than made any sense at all. I have been lying to myself, but have been thrown off the track of admitting my powerlessness over alcohol by the fact that I often go without it.

I drink to let go of my internal need to be in control, and sometimes I actually relax enough to experience some fun. Rarely, though, do I feel real joy.

So here I am. I want to be cured of my pain. I cannot endure my feelings that have peaked in this year: that I am a Loser. My life is out of control, and all of the years of keeping everything and everyone together have built to this moment. I am incredibly sad. I am feeling more alone than I ever have in my life. I need to understand why I allowed myself to get into this situation.

There are about twenty people in this spare, strange building that is to be my home for the next month. I was scared when I walked into the dining room, sort of a first-day-at-school feeling, only worse. What the fuck have I mismanaged to find myself here?

I dread the weekend. The other patients are friendly,

but I want to get into the difficult part of the work, and not have to be sociable on this first, visitorless weekend.

Day 2 — If only I could let go of my compulsive, often sexual, need to make up for my own void. I am given something to read—the institute is constantly giving us homework—and I am stunned to realize that my compulsion is sometimes controllable in the alcohol department, but not in the sexual area. I am desperate to be held, to be convinced that I am worth loving. And while I honestly believe that I love in return with more than my share, I am starting to question my motives.

I have just had a long swim in the evening light with some new friends. We alcoholics seem dreary compared to the drug addicts. My on-again, off-again, (I'll-admit-it-tonight) mostly on-again alcohol habit was my choice for a slow and disgusting death. No furtive border runs with five kilos of cocaine. I used to convince myself that some shots of tequila were very macho. Hot stuff. Pioneer woman.

Bullshit.

I am relieved to know that I shall get up at tomorrow night's meeting and say the words: "My name is Ali and I am an alcoholic." I had wondered how I would ever be able to say that, but now I can't wait. I look constantly at my blue plastic bracelet: I am in a hospital! Unbelievable! I am a very sick person, and I need treatment! I fooled everyone, including myself, with achievement and style and "niceness." I feel like the biggest phony on earth, and I have to force myself to remember that underneath all this facade I believe there is a decent and genuine human being. Right now I'm not sure who is going to hatch from this egg, and I am scared.

I know what I want to be: honest. Really honest. Vulnerable, loving, but not needy of being validated by love. What a bad deal for someone to get close to me these past years. It seemed good, but my behavior has been fraudulent and manipulative. I've done just about everything to be liked and loved, to be made to feel whole. In fact I have been a hollow, insecure, empty cardboard tube, papering myself with achievements and unsatisfying friendships, just to pretend to myself that I am whole.

Day 3 — I worry about being discovered here by the *National Enquirer* or some other trash magazine. They have been tracking me for years. Everyone here needs, and is entitled to, privacy and confidentiality, but I know that Ali MacGraw would be a juicy name to drop in the gossip columns. Somewhere in a dead photo file there will be a picture of me blowing my nose with the flu, suitable illustration for a sensational article—"Career in Ruins, Love Life Over, She Turns to Alcohol."

I was supposed to be checked again by the nurse this morning (stick out my tongue and see if my hands shake), and so I rushed out of bed at 6:00 A.M., only to learn that they had decided I didn't need to see her. I was suddenly terribly depressed at the prospect of a whole empty Sunday ahead of me. I just could not pull myself out of my loneliness and futility. That turned out to be a feeling shared by at least one other patient, "Jack," about whom I am really concerned. I have never seen such agony in anyone's eyes, and when he says he is afraid that there is "nothing to him" inside all his barriers and chemicals and pain, I am speechless. My own pain seems somewhat insignificant, but I must remember that I am here because I, too, have bottomed out.

My usual trick in the past has been to get right into another person's problems, thus avoiding tackling my own. Only now do I realize that this whole maneuver was a device to make me feel powerful: they are the ones with a problem. I am Good Girl, the Everybody-Likes-You Girl.

I have made the choice all my life of going for Perfect, even if it has been constipating and joyless. When is the last time I experienced real, true joy? Only in bed, I'm afraid, and that's probably why I am so desperate for that particular connection. If I can fall in love, and then make love (or maybe it is the other way around), I experience at least a facsimile of joy.

I also was drinking to loosen up, drinking because at least there was the possibility of forcing a relaxation and perhaps encountering joy. I am beginning to realize that it wasn't joy; it was hysteria.

Today, I feel safer and more curious being with my fellow patients. We talk at the oddest times, and stop to exchange what I consider to be life-and-death intimacies.

I want to do hard, hard work while I am here, and hopefully gain a true sense that I can triumph over this emotional illness before I expose myself to the outside world and all the old stuff again. I want to be stripped down to my real, long-lost center and see it, and learn to value it before I share it with anyone outside of here. I cannot bear to present myself one more time as the phony performer who pretends to be okay.

I want to fly.

Day 4 — This morning "Dominic," who is in my group, asked some of us if we would give our honest opinions of him. I said that all I could see was a very open and really sweet man—almost like a child, in the best sense. We took a little walk and he described in detail his free-base habit: the ritual, the money, the danger, the guns, the land-of-Mafia drama of it all, followed by what everyone has already told me is the greatest euphoric drug high of them all. I was struck by something: it seems to me that the free-base users have an added pressure on their recovery, and that is, how do you duplicate the pure, dangerous adventure of the cocaine game? Most of us alcoholics just slide into degradation and loss of self-esteem. The only physical danger to ourselves is a health matter. We lack the "rush" of the drug game. I wonder how many drug victims can start their new lives with a newfound gratifying rush to equal not only the specific drug high but also the game itself?

Everyone seemed to feel very much happier today, perhaps the result of Sunday being over. I think that if I had had my choice, I would never have checked in on a Friday, with the weekend yawning empty before me. I feel much better jumping right into the work. I am dying to get at the core of my behavior. I feel as if I have been through every possible route of exploration and have come up with no answers, and this is my last shot.

Dr. West gave a lecture tonight. What hair-raising statistics he gave us: the death rate among alcoholics, for example. The enormity of this illness astonished me. I feel as though I arrived here just in time to save my life. I am so grateful to my friends who convinced me to come.

And to God. I sense the beginnings of an understanding of a Higher Power, and that makes me happy.

Daily, nightly, although I have not needed to weep about it since I arrived here, I wonder about my future in terms of a mate. It upsets me to realize that for the first time since Steve, I have made a real commitment to share my life, yet I fear that I have made a totally hopeless choice in Ben.

I am not only compulsive but I am consistent in my wrong choices. Just when I felt ready at last to be open in a relationship, I again involved myself with someone whose priorities are different from mine. My big wish for when I leave here is to have peace of mind in terms of Ben.

Day 5 — I learned something today. I have noticed how much the cocaine addicts glamorize their lives and problems, and all of a sudden something snapped within me. I was furious. If these people cannot show the pain and terror that I feel, why should I make naked my pain in the hope of learning from this experience? In near tears I kept saying that I could not stand the fact that the alcoholic, female especially, is perceived to be a slatternly pig, while the coke addict is often pictured as a kind of exciting, danger-courting renegade.

Now that I've calmed down, I thank them: you made me remember the terrible, terrible, terrible pain I've felt as an alcoholic. You made me realize how much bullshit I've been laying on all these years, the charm and energy and half truth that I've used to mask my agony. I am afraid that I hurt some of their feelings (and that is not purely about "Please, everyone—like me"). Maybe I busted one of them as I need someone to bust me. Mostly I shocked myself into realizing just how ill I have been, and I am very clear about what work I have to do.

I also talked to my roommate, "Janet," who still looks in terrible torment. She has touched me with the unbelievable, almost ritualistic sense of order she gives to our room. I feel for her quandary about facing life as a widow, starting life over again. She has planned to stay in the area for a while with her grandchildren to put off the inevitable confrontation with the same old life. That of course plugs me into the subject to which we all relate: will I be okay when I'm away from this extraordinary support community? I go from one extreme to another, from self-assurance to utter terror.

It is 9:30 in the evening, and I am alone on the patio, with a half moon and stars and crickets and stillness for a change. It gets rowdy here at night, and as much as I would love to laugh and carry on with the rest of them, most of all I long to get my work done.

One person told me tonight that laughter was practically prescribed for her to help with the long comedown from barbiturates. So many of my new friends are laughing and being jolly. At best I feel strong (that is my "happy" mood swing). I never, ever feel at ease. When I catch myself in the mirror, I see a rigid and sad face trying to look comfortable and pleasant. In order to feel joy I need to begin loosening my grip on all this control. It hasn't happened yet.

Day 6 — Today was the hardest day I have had here. I was nailed for my lifelong need to control—and here I am trying to control exactly when I will arrive at a sense of that spiritual awareness which will make the rest of my life okay. I am so impatient, so scared to death that I want to get out of my own way, turn off my brain, and let it all just happen. I started to cry, and the more scared I got, the harder I cried.

It was not until I saw the psychiatrist later in the day that I had a big revelation about control. For the first time in all my life and after many analysts, I realized that the role I played as a child at home was that of the controller. As Daddy was less angry with me than he was with my brother, I took on the part of the Good Little Girl who was going to cajole him into a better mood when I saw his rage building toward a beating. I also watched over my brother to keep him from deliberately tempting disaster. I was the controller to prevent terrifying violence, and I made it a full-time job while I was living with my parents. Little did I realize that as an adult this same contrived behavior—trying to make everything all right—only reinforced my uptight, judgmental personality.

Well, that is a big one.

I have a new roommate now, "Natasha." We share certain details of our alcoholism, such as our tight, Perfect presentation. We are also similar in our shame at losing our dignity, particularly in front of our children.

Day 7 — The moon is nearly full, and the stars are out. I would love to sit outside in silence and dream, but I will probably just stay in bed until Natasha comes in, and I can watch her remarkable ritual. I miss Janet: her blunt, sweet honesty and carefully worked-out way of living were very comforting and nice to be around. Now, the room has been turned into a homey, detailed reflection of Natasha's very different life style. It is all photographs and flowers and books and candles and Porthault linens and more matching pieces of luggage than I would take to go around the world. I like her, though. There is even a bowl of Gummi Bears, set out like a hostess's offering. In our sugar-craving fever, we demolish them every ten hours, and generously she always replaces them. She's very dependent upon her material props, and yet when I see all those photographs of her, thinner and very attractive, I wonder if pain and self-loathing might have allowed her to put on so much weight. It is as though those pictures were a reminder.

One of the precepts of recovery is that we must make "a decision to turn our will and our lives over to the care of God as we understand Him." I have wanted so badly to have an idea of how to turn my will and my life over to a Higher Power, as I call it, and I have not known how. Today Father Frank said that the Higher Power could be, on the simplest level, the combined, positive power of our group; that somehow, by some "coincidence," we were all led here to save our lives; that somehow the Higher Power works for us through other people. And suddenly I felt an enormous weight leave my back. I am ecstatic because I begin to understand, finally, that there has to be a God guiding me, through the people who care for my well-being at this moment and, I hope, for the rest of my life. I was astounded at the simple way this explanation was made and at the relief it brings me. (It was interesting that the two diehard Catholics in our group were furious afterward.)

One woman told her story today: anger so close to my own that I became undone. It is inconceivable that such a gentle soul has ever done any of the horrific and angry things that she recounts. I felt in some ways that she was telling almost my exact life story, and it was devastating.

There is someone new here who has not said anything, but he surprised me this afternoon by busting me for my judgmental attitude. He said he was disappointed in my gossipy comment about someone in line at breakfast, that he had not thought I was "that kind of person." I was very ashamed of my remark and glad to be called on it. I want so badly to let go of all my bad stuff—to let go, period. I need all the help I can get.

Day 8 — I can't believe I have been here a whole week. I cannot focus clearly on what my daily life was like before I arrived, but I remember crying every day for what seemed like hours, and feeling nothing but a sense of utter loss. Now I cry at the drop of a hat, but I have a small inkling that I can fill up my emptiness; at least I get flashes of that. Then suddenly, very schizophrenically, I ache for what I thought I had with Ben and I feel unbearably lonely and sad. The mood swing takes so little time that it leaves me exhausted.

Every day I have a new piece of information that sinks forever into my mind, and tiny though it may or may not be, I know that it is part of a jigsaw puzzle. That puzzle is mostly blank right now, but a week ago it was totally empty. I know that all the pieces will fit, and that patience and paying attention to detail will eventually make the puzzle complete.

Day 11 — When I walk into the next relationship with a man, I want to be a little more wary, a lot less needy, and surer that I am Somebody—not to throw myself away and then feel sorry for the mess I've made.

Day 12 — I was glad to hear a friendly voice on the phone today. I called Alan Nierob because his is the phone number I had left on my answering service in case someone called regarding business. I had told him I was going to a friend's cabin in Montana, to write; that's the story I gave out to everyone. He was glad I called with the truth because he would have been upset to hear through the Hollywood grapevine that I had been admitted here. And as my press agent he would have had to deal with it. I owed him the truth.

In the most masochistic way, I asked about Ben. He said that I should forget him, that Ben was not in a very monogamous mood these days. I am starting to realize that I cannot worry about and invent the future, that I have to stay only in the present.

I don't fear that I might drink again as much as I fear the terrible depressions, and what will happen if I get smacked around too much when I try to come back. I hope that the real world is ready for the amount of hand-holding and hugging I need. Although that has a victim-y ring, I try to prepare myself for the behavior that is an integral part of our culture.

I believe in God, now more than ever, and in honesty and in right and wrong. This morning I decided that I am being punished for being involved with a married man, for my part in hurting his ex-wife.

I feel so much better after my six o'clock swim. One

big revelation: I realize something about my son, Joshua. I have been subtly telling him: "I don't trust you. Be perfect *my* way." That is what I got from my parents, and particularly from my mother. I shall never forget that her very first comment to me, upon learning that I had been chosen for the lead in *Goodbye, Columbus,* was not "How wonderful; we are proud of you," but "I hope it doesn't go to your head." It is hard to separate my real love and respect for her from other feelings: that she was prissy, humorless, stand-apart judgmental, and martyrish. All this in the most powerful, resourceful female I have ever known. And she was good. When I see myself from outside, I see so many things we have in common, but some of them I cannot stand. It makes me angry. I will not allow myself to become like her in those ways. Luckily for Josh, he is not afraid to tell me how he feels.

I rescued a little frog from the pool this morning. He sat on my hand awhile before he hopped off into the zinnias. As I looked at the beautiful sunrise, all alone in the pool, me and my frog, I thought, "Hmm, tomorrow he might turn into Robert Redford."

Day 13 — There was a terrifying lecture this morning about the half life of sedatives, and all I could think of was the contents of a certain friend's medicine chest. That plus a lot of cocaine and alcohol add up to severe danger. I pray that some of my new education can help him before his addiction kills him.

Day 14 — Like everyone else here, I had to tell my "autobiography" today. Because I have had to tell my life story in minute detail so many times in the last sixteen years I was scared that it was going to be perceived as a tired and fake performance. I am a little sick of the details, and so maybe the telling will lack the freshness of a first-time revelation; but I absolutely own my own story. I realize that alcohol is not my only disease, that male dependency has made me as dysfunctional and ashamed and out of control as the other. I am scared that the group does not realize how seriously I take this—that they think I treat it all too casually. I am so frustrated that I want to cry.

I got an assignment. I am to write a letter to myself evaluating what I see.

Dear Alice:

I need to call you "Alice" to remind you what a perfect, prissy little girl you are: perfect grades, perfect manners, critical, judgmental, superior, smug, rule-following, crowd-pleasing perfect. Nothing to be so proud of.

Alice: it might have been better if you had had the courage to break some of the little rules long ago, instead of saving up for the big ones when you were older and no longer living at home. I am angry at you for so many reasons, I only hope I can name them all: you have made my life lonely and miserable.

Your overachievement and intelligence and ability to cope on a certain level have earned you prizes and applause and press and so-called fame, and none of that made you happy at all. Why didn't you have the guts to admit and confront your alcoholism fifteen years ago, instead of wasting irretrievable years with doctors who flattered your intelligence and didn't help you deal with your feelings?

You know what? I believe you liked the way you could manipulate yourself and others with your intelligence, and stay far away from your feelings in the process. It made you feel a little superior, didn't it?

You asshole.

You shortchanged yourself with that super-subtle manipulation: you pretended to be "dealing," and you were just wasting half your life, wallowing in the long-ago facts of your garbage. I cannot get back those forty-seven years, and I am furious. You have robbed me, and I hope I can learn to forgive you/me.

Do you want specifics? When you were little you never once had the courage to stand up to the only two grown-ups you ever had to deal with in that constipated home: your parents. Why didn't you scream at your father, attack him physically if necessary, to shock him into laying off of you and especially your brother? And why did you watch your mother stand by and not protect you two children? Don't you hate yourself now for the invention you are, a cross between the "mysterious intellectual"—or the pseudo-intellectual/artist your father pretended to be—and the stoic mother who tended the so-called genius she needed her husband to be? You've been playing both parts, Alice, for years: the martyred guardian of your own specialness, with no joy, no freedom, no sensuality allowed.

Unless, of course, you are drunk. Then out comes the dancing, laughing, overeating, irresponsible you, the one you lie about enjoying. Well, don't lie to me, Alice: I know very well how ashamed you are of so much of your promiscuous, immoral behavior, and I hate you for putting yourself into this position. You were brought up with ethics and honesty and decency and real values. How do you feel about adultery and false flattery and manipulation and popularity contests and lying to your child?

You have honestly tried to be a good mother, and the world in which you have chosen to work has, like many worlds, sometimes made that difficult. Do you think that going to soccer matches and the PTA, and even talking honestly with your son about his and your feelings has made up for the lying you have done to him about your irrational behavior and your disease? I hate you for shortchanging the greatest gift you'll ever have—and hope it's not too late. I'll kill you if it is.

Sure, there were sad and lonely, abnormal things in your childhood: it's not normal, Alice, to have parents who were social hermits, who never ever touched each other, or hugged, or invited friends to supper—or even cultivated many friendships. By now, you know enough to forgive them, because you understand why they acted as they did. But listen: that's your fucking intelligence getting in the way, as usual. It has never helped to make you happy before, and it won't now. There were some ugly and lonely things about your childhood, and you hurt, and you were very angry and frightened from the very earliest moment—why didn't you begin to deal with it then? Why haven't you dealt with your anger and disgust with yourself as it has come along, instead of storing it all up and ruining everything?

I think you are a fraud. You throw around your judgments, tell half truths so that people will like you, and court men, in particular, with lying promises of who you are and what you want, just so you won't be alone. You disgust me.

You have wasted half of your life by selecting these unfulfilling relationships. Just how much time do you think you have to squander away? You are not the wonderful, giving, arty bohemian you pretend to be; you are pretty deadly. You trap people with your manipulative charm, and then, after your lies have become a life-style, you begin to boil inside and fester, until the alcohol (which you so cleverly drink on the sly) brings out all your deep rage and hurt and ugliness.

You behave disgracefully, and I am ashamed of you. You have behaved insensitively toward the women whose husbands you have slept with, and you should know better than that; you've had it done to you, and you didn't like it. And you've disrespected most of the men you have been with, with that bullshit excuse to yourself: "having to do it to them before they do it to you." Why have you sold yourself short and then behaved in such a cheap and common fashion?

You are wounded and angry that most people don't seem to know and respect you for—as you put it— "who you are." Well, who the fuck are you, anyway?

You'll have to stand up and show us, Alice, before it's too late. You'll have to run the risk that we might not love you, or even like you. So what?

Has your manipulation and so-called charm and all that terror made you happy?

Have any of those so-called achievements and prizes made you happy?

*Has your hollow smile and spiritual detachment
made you happy?*

*You know they haven't. I am angry that you have
run your life so terribly, and I am telling you that you
have run out of time.*

*And more than anything, I am angry that your
behavior can make me angry. I am tired of this ugliness,
Alice. I want to be happy.*

Day 15 — I got up in the meeting tonight when it came
time for me to say who I was, and I said, "My name is
Ali, and I am an Alcoholic/Male Dependent."

I really feel that it is the other way around, but my
counselor had suggested that I identify myself that way
and I cannot describe the relief I feel in naming and
owning the disease.

The people in my group, and most of the people here,
give me so much. I am overwhelmed with the love and
caring, and I think that I have a standard for what I need
from a real friend or mate. If I can't have the intimacy
and trust that I've found here in two weeks, maybe I will
have to rebuild my life around others in recovery.

Day 16 — My first meditative journey to the Wise Man.

I am walking on a soft dirt path, barefoot. On either
side of it are deep violet flowers with peculiar cactuslike
leaves. This desert is rich in plants. The moon is pale
and enormous, the sky deep gray and pricked with stars.
It is very still, and I would be having a wonderful walk
if I were not terrified of snakes. I cannot take a step
without looking everywhere in anticipation of seeing a
huge rattlesnake. I am paralyzed with fear, when sud-

denly I see a primitive white sign lettered in black: NO SNAKES. Wonderful! Now I can have a leisurely walk and smell the perfumed air.

I pass four very alert jackrabbits, lined up like a regiment, eyes on me. I sense that they are a sort of guidepost for me to notice on the way in and out of this place. I see a narrow, steep path just ahead to the right, and I take it. I climb up toward the top, and notice that the terrain has changed—no more vegetation, except for occasional clumps of desert gray-green grass. The earth turns to beige shingle—rocks and shale.

Ahead of me I can see a small cave, a hole in a mound of earth and stones. There is one tree, a very dusty-leafed poplar, and a hammock. The ground around the home is dust.

There is a small bonfire to my left, and I sit down beside it. Across from me, across from the little fire, sits the Wise Man. His face has no age, just the hundreds of wrinkles and deep nut color of a life in the desert sun. His eyes, brilliant and piercing blue, are staring at me. His mouth, which is difficult for me to see through the flames of the fire, seems to be a slight, pleasant smile. He has the body of a wonderfully fit man in his late twenties and his hands have long, elegant fingers.

I ask him a question: "Where is happiness?"

He answers, "Inside you."

I become him. As the Wise Man, I stretch out my fingers and trace rainbow cellophane ribbons around in an arc over me, the Pilgrim.

I, the Pilgrim, take the rainbows and wrap them around me, over and over. I can see through them to the Wise Man behind the fire. What I know about the Wise

Man is that he plays with the rainbow ribbons, ritualistically, like a martial arts dancer, slowly and languidly, every morning. When he sees a pilgrim making his way up the mountain, he signals for silence. His lessons are in silence.

He gives me a present from the worn leather pouch in back of him. He fumbles around and pulls out a small sienna-colored, finger-worn amulet, a gift for me. It is a cross—not a long-stemmed Catholic cross, but a squarer one. Many hands have held it. I feel them.

I walk back down the hill, fingering my gift and my yards and yards of rainbow. I pass my four jackrabbits, and know I'm on the right path. Suddenly I come upon a huge green meadow, damp with dew and studded with fat yellow flowers. All around me are pale lavender mountains, slightly snowcapped. I lie down in the grass and clover, and wind up my rainbow ribbon so that I can carry it better. I rub the cross on my stomach, and after some moments of silence, I continue on my way again, holding my two treasures tightly in my fist.

Day 17 — I have been here two weeks, and the single biggest thing that has happened to me is my newfound certainty that there is a Higher Power. I shall call it God. I am beginning to feel an underlying peace and sense of order that I have yearned for forever.

I know He brought me here to begin my real life with my real self, at long, long last.

Day 18 — I still have lots of questions about the specific details of most organized religions, but I am wholly convinced of God as the Higher Power. When I used to say

that "there are no accidents," I guess I was getting closer
to the realization that I have a Higher Power that guides
me every step of my life.

The lesson at the church service reminded me again
of the very terrible thing that I have done: adultery. I
have been unfaithful to almost every man I have been
with.

At the same time, I am embarrassed that I continue to
worry about the prospect of months ahead without sex.

Day 19 — Today it was my turn to be evaluated by the
whole group, their observations, pro and con, put up on
a blackboard for all to see. After it ended I felt like a rag
doll, with my torso bashed in and the wood shavings
falling out of my legs. I fear that I will not be able to put
myself back together again. I know I have to, but I don't
know where to begin. I don't know how to walk, how
to act, who I really am. How ironic that I had written
one of my few optimistic notes in my journal last night,
and here I am at noon feeling as though I have to start
my whole life over. I am exhausted.

There was nothing new in the criticisms and observations of the group, but it hurts to be confronted by all
the things I have hated about myself. One comment that
flattened me today was to hear myself described as "California Cuisine." What does that mean? Decorative with
no insides? Healthy, but chi-chi? "California Cuisine"
sounds fake and empty to me.

It reminded me of something that happened at
Wellesley. My favorite professor was a sculptor and a
graphic artist, and more than anything I wanted him
to respect my work. (I think I wanted to emulate his

whole life; I even named my son after his baby.) One day when we were working on designs for a record jacket for Carl Orff's *Carmina Burana,* he stopped to look at my work and said, sarcastically, "Ah, yes, Ali— I can see you, years from now, the big editor of *Flair* [a trendy, short-lived magazine]. You will have long nails and you will be wearing a big emerald ring and 'directing' everything." For years I loathed the color green, but more importantly, his remark exacerbated an already present fear: that I would somehow be considered a fake—a flashy bit of luck, nothing more.

I feel like shit.

But I am a fighter, and I am going to put myself back together in a better way. Right now I just don't know quite how.

Day 20 — My Life. What a great, great, great gift. I'll have to fumble around to get it.

Sometimes I am rushing a thousand miles an hour, headed somewhere on a road. Everything is so much in the past, and what I am experiencing now has the urgency of life and death. I am on a wild carnival ride, which means fun and scary, all in one.

Whatever "insane" is, I sometimes think I must be that, but in most ways it feels a lot better than what I was before: "dead."

Today we were all assembled in the dining room to learn how to meditate. We were told to stare out of the window until our eyes focused on one spot, and then to allow ourselves to become totally absorbed in it. My eyes took in the flowering shrubs and the landscape and then the mountains surrounding Palm Springs. Gradually they discovered the side of one mountain, violet in the deep shadow of one side, and brilliant with sun on the top plateau. My mind drifted, the image before me growing more abstract. From somewhere deep in my subconscious I found myself remembering the Twenty-third Psalm, where it says, "Though I walk through the valley of the shadow of death, I shall fear no evil. For Thou art with me" . . . and suddenly I knew in my heart that I had indeed passed through the valley of the shadow of death, and that I was safe at last. I was no longer alone. Here at the treatment center, I had finally made a spiritual connection with my Higher Power.

I had a terrible, terrible dream: "Graduation" from here was a test, a huge tightrope of twisted net strung 500 feet over a cement floor. When my turn came I was wearing net gloves, and my hands kept slipping, and I felt that I was going to fall. I was petrified. "Maggie," one of our group, kept smiling her beautiful smile and saying, "You'll make it."

Day 22 — The sense of time here is so peculiar. At first the days crept by interminably, and while I never once thought about leaving early, it sometimes felt as though I'd never finish the program. Now I am turning the corner into my final week, and the days rush by. I have moments when I cannot wait to go home and be with my animals and my garden and, more than anything else, with Josh. But there are times when I look carefully at everything here, and I wish I could stay, safe and protected forever. I feel myself detaching a little bit, too, and I wonder if that is like the teenage kid who begins to break away from his parents. Or is it my old alcoholic loneliness again?

The mixture of the group has changed from a lot of cocaine addicts to a large proportion of older alcoholic women. They remind me of myself if I don't work my program every single day, and they scare me to death. It's no accident that they are here in my final week: they are a warning.

I see how hard it will be to replace the intimacy that is the standard of behavior here, and I understand why my friend Lynda told me recently that she was going to be looking for all new friends. I don't know about *all* new friends, but I know that I will have to rethink some of my relationships. In my education these short few weeks I have enjoyed a kind of total honesty and vulnerability with perfect strangers, and I realize that in many cases it is more intimate than anything I have with many of my "old friends." It makes me sad to realize that some of us may be growing apart.

Over the years, I have had certain friends who have been uncomfortable with my growing celebrity. They assumed that my insides had changed, and that I needed to be treated differently because of my job. That has hurt my feelings. Now, I have a new dilemma: how do I make my friends understand that even when I am happy, and my life seems to be in perfect order, I am one of those people who cannot have just one glass of wine? I wish I could. There is a common misunderstanding that the chemical or brain malfunction—which is addiction—goes away with the tough days. That is simply not so. Apparently we alcoholics and addicts are somehow wired up differently from other people. But an equally important lesson is one that I have to learn: that real friendship demands lack of control and judgment. When I look back on my friendships over the years I have to admit with some shame that I have very often presented myself as open and available and loving, only to pull back into myself as the person dared to be close to me. And for fear of disapproval I have rarely had the courage to say what displeases me in another person, because it has taken me all this time to realize that that can be done without anger or disapproval.

Among all the people I have considered to be my friends over the years, there are very few whom I have allowed to see the real me. One who comes to mind, though, is the painter Barbara Nessim, whom I have known since my stylist days in New York. Had I really been paying attention all these years I could have learned a lot about support and unconditional love from her. Miraculously, she seems to have been honest and non-manipulative since the beginning, while I feel as though I have just begun to know what it takes to be a real friend. I know that there are other people, too, whom I can really count on in a crisis. It amazes me that in life the most unexpected people sometimes are the ones who throw you the life preserver—old friends like Dory Previn and Joby Baker, and new ones like Jeff Wald and Jeff Campbell. I am grateful to have had my eyes opened before it was too late, and I pray for the courage to be more honest with everyone.

I feel as though someone (myself) put me on a big empty raft and pushed me way out into the middle of a beautiful mountain lake, to watch the sun and the trees and those mountains, in perfect stillness. And now my raft is drifting by itself, to shore. I don't know which shore, and I am not sure who will be there. But I know that sooner or later, very slowly, my raft is going to bump softly against a sandy little bank, and there will be at least a few people in the woods who will come out to welcome me. God has already planned that.

Day 23 — I thought of my mother today. I had a vision of her standing in the kitchen, blue-gray skirt, blue-gray and salmon plaid shirt, and the silver fish pin with a topaz belly that Daddy had designed. She was much smaller than I, but with big shoulders like mine, and lean from a lot of physical work. Her salt-and-pepper hair was pulled back in a bun, and she wore only a little lipstick, nothing more. Her body was rigid with the tension of too much to do. The more I looked into her face, the sadder I became. She never got her share of affection and compliments for all the remarkable things she did for us. I cried and cried for her today, for her not being here so that I could hold her and tell her how wonderful she was.

And Daddy? I visualized him standing by the horrible mahogany sideboard in the living room of the house we rented. He was clutching the edge, gasping for breath because of the terror of his emphysema. As always, he was freshly shaved and immaculately dressed, and he looked at me kind of sideways, with gentleness and rage at the same time. I felt how much he needed to be loved. He had had a lonely and scary childhood, and was never sure he was worth anything, and I just wanted him to know that I loved and valued him very much.

We all four—my brother, our parents, and I—cheated

ourselves and one another by not reaching out and holding each other, through all those difficult years. I feel like a real child now, and very vulnerable and in need of having parents and laughter and protection. I know I can, and will, take care of myself, but I wish someone else would care for me right now, while I heal.

When I looked back into my past to find joy and serenity and hope, I had to look all the way back to college, to a photograph taken of me on the stone steps looking out over a beautiful New England lake, with the whole world before me. I remember how proud my parents were of me and how free and strong I felt. I had friends at last, and the soaring feeling that nothing could keep me from my bright future.

Day 24 — I had a disturbing realization today. In contemplating my fantasy of Ben, I am forced to acknowledge my own contribution to the problem. I admit to manipulation, jealousy of his peers for the time and passion he gave them, need for control and power over his priorities, and the inexcusable act of making him question his own value and his work. And when I finish that list and make the list of what I loved about him, I come up with something I haven't felt in a while: terrible loneliness for the moments that were good. I wish that my admission and honest apology for my behavior in the past six months would make the problems go away, and find him loving me again. I know this is not healthy.

Day 25 — I feel frustrated to be returning home to the realities of my life: Josh's month with his father; the necessity of work; alcoholism meetings and hours of driving to get to them—and no evidence of a male companion. It embarrasses me to admit the latter, but the burden of my aloneness is also sexual. I miss being held. I wish I could share my feelings with a man who would understand, and would also give me that other affection that I absolutely need to be happy.

Day 26 — A friend called to say that she had talked to Josh for more than an hour today, and that he was very upset and really needed me. I called the goddam Evans mansion, and the butler, after stumbling around, said he couldn't find Josh. That business used up my allotted fifteen minutes of telephone time, so all I could do was to leave a message saying that I loved and missed him terribly, and to please be home about 7:30 tomorrow so that we could talk.

I have been away for four weeks, and Josh has been with his father the whole time. Josh, now fifteen, who is so incredibly smart and perceptive, has bought into a dangerous dream. He has allowed himself to imagine that once I come home, clean and sober, we shall all be together again as a family. It makes me angry and sad that he sees me as the sole dysfunctional in this group. It doesn't help to realize that he is like every other child of divorced parents. Even eight years after the divorce, he continues to hope that we will all be together. I feel so helpless.

Day 27 — Something happened this afternoon that made me angry. A number of us were sitting together, and we were joined by a counselor who had made me really uncomfortable since the very beginning. She said fliply, "I have a Ph.D. in Drink." I said, "And I have a Ph.D. in Bullshit." Then she said, "I have two words for you: 'Lighten up.'"

Lighten up? How the hell am I expected to crash right past this major transition in my life and get light, just like that?

I talked to Josh tonight. He sounded so grown up. He is most anxious that he can count on being with me alone all weekend "to talk." I am a little nervous. He said that he has had a wonderful, important month while I have been away. That can only mean a celebration of the Beverly Hills life-style.

Day 28 — I have "graduated" and I am on my way home. However, I have made a terrible mistake. I wanted to rent a car and drive myself back home after the Medallion ceremony, but I was so shaky I was afraid of the several hours on the freeway. I thought about having a car pick me up, but I didn't want to tell a limousine service to meet me at a treatment center—and I was idiotically embarrassed at the idea that anyone at the center might think I was doing a movie star turn. The only solution seemed to be for me to catch a ride back with two other people who had finished treatment at the same time I did, and it was a terrible mistake. I have been trapped in their car all afternoon: rock and roll and teenage loudness that totally jangled my already fragile nerves. Worse still, I am stuck in a condominium in God-knows-what desert community between Palm Springs and L.A. All the lights are on, and two televisions, too, and I want to scream. As well-meaning as these people are, I really can't relate to them. I am desperate to GO HOME. The confines of the Center fooled me, made me forget what I really need: quiet and privacy and close friends.

I will pretend that my first day "out" is tomorrow.

I am determined to stay sober, and to hang on to the sense of serenity. I shall read my little meditation books, write, go to meetings, and most of all, spend time with friends.

A t home, day 1 — It feels so good to be back in my beach house again, with my animals leaping with excitement to see me at last, and the deck a riot of summer geraniums. Julia has filled my home with order, and with fresh-cut flowers, and the refrigerator with my favorite salad makings. Best of all, there is Josh. I feel lonely and scared nonetheless. God must be putting me through this pain to prepare me for the rest of my life. It's been six weeks and a day since I left Ben, and life sure does go on. How long can this pain last? I feel nothing, and yet I ache. It doesn't make sense. I want to cry. I'm scared, all over again. I am alone. All over again.

An old friend called and wants to see me soon. He said we should do something dramatic like take the Concorde to London and have Indian food. I'd like to; I would particularly like Ben to cringe at my seeing another man.

Especially this one: he is really *attractive*. What a stupid, pointless sentiment! Once again I am feeling *unattractive*. It will be very difficult at my age to meet a man who is both exciting and honorable.

I wish Josh wanted to move far away from this Hollywood orbit, but he told me today that he wanted to move from Malibu to Bel Air! When I dropped him at Bob's house I saw how dependent he has become on his father. It upset me that Bob gets all this unconditional loyalty and passion. Sometimes I feel as though all my time and planning has been taken for granted, but then I stop to realize how important it is for Josh and Bob to love each other, and they do. And through all the years of turmoil, one of the real miracles of my life is how loyal and loving a family we have managed to remain. But I looked at photos of Josh today and was repelled to see how many were studied, intense, smileless. What is Bob trying to turn Josh into? What happened to my child? I long for Josh's happier, less troubled, more innocent face.

Serenity is hard for me to find today.

Day 3 — Thank goodness I went into treatment at the Betty Ford Center. Thank goodness I found a fellowship of people who share my illness and my feelings. Thank goodness I am sober. Thank goodness I believe in my Higher Power. Today I had proof that made me know that my life is indeed starting over. Very matter-of-factly, Jerry Breslauer informed me that the house I rent has been sold, and unless I can come up with $1.4 million this week to buy it, I shall have to leave at the end of

May. I was devastated. I love my home, even though I do not own it; we have been here ten years. Where will we live? Josh is very excited about moving, but for me it is heartbreaking. This place has given me security. Jerry went on with the news that I would have to change my life-style drastically, that I would have to sell some things in order to live, because no income is forthcoming. I count on Jerry to tell me the truth, but this was bad news.

It is about time I got in touch with my rage at Steve for making me give up a career in order to be his wife, and for making me sign a prenuptial agreement. The real fury is directed at myself, however, for thinking so little of my own worth that I signed it. I am not a victim here, I must remember. All day I muttered about how God must be planning to take everything away in order for me to make a new life.

I wish Ben would lose all his hair, soon.

Day 4 — More and more I am grateful that I was brought to my knees. I am being tested to the maximum these days, and I know that it is God's design. The accumulation of things that are being taken away is no coincidence: no lover, no job, no house. Something astonishing must be in store for me.

The panic has subsided, and for the moment I feel stronger and more serene.

Tonight I walked from one end of the beach to the other, looking wistfully for a house for Josh and me. I love this beach—the privacy, the dunes, the comparative lack of people. Josh can always stay with his father, but where will I go?

I went to a local meeting tonight and shared what is going on in my life. Afterward I was strangely elated. I felt attractive, clear-eyed, and powerful; this program really does work.

Things are looking up. I now have a couple of scripts to read, a couple of possibilities for work.

Suddenly, however, I feel estranged from Josh. He is negative, judgmental, and lost. I don't like what's going on at his father's house: the values, priorities, lack of schedule. But I am pretty powerless over it. Josh is so good that it breaks my heart to see him like this, and I know I am partly responsible. I miss my "little boy."

Day 5 — Finally, I had a good conversation with Joshua. It took until two o'clock in the morning, but I feel much better about our relationship. He says he worries most of all about whether I am lonely or sad. He worries when I leave him at his dad's that I have nowhere to go, no one to see. I reassured him that hard as it might be for him to understand, I am much happier, and that there is nothing to worry about.

Day 8 — It has been almost thirty-nine days since I stopped drinking, and ten more since the Breakup. That's a long time without sexuality or even hugs. I have been told by my counselors that I should not get embroiled in a man-woman situation for at least a year, and this is depressing and horrifying.

Josh joined me and Bob for dinner tonight. Josh looked extra-chic and handsome, but he was silent the whole time. Bob was extremely uncomfortable when I tried to tell him about the dangers of all the prescription drugs that he has taken all these years. I tried to tell him some of the things I had learned in treatment, but he didn't want to hear. We also talked about Josh while he was away from the table for a minute. Bob was firm in his belief that Josh's peculiar and sad behavior is only because he is an adolescent boy with no luck with the ladies. Bob is completely unaware of what I see as his overuse of Joshua as Best Friend/Confidant. He stubbornly continues to see Joshua as the son of two Hollywood stars, locked in the ordinary problems of divorce, fame, and only-son predicaments. My recent education tells me it is not that simple.

Day 9 — I went to see a house this afternoon. The property overlooks the ocean and there are wonderful trees and a garden; I know just what to do to make the little house spectacular. Tomorrow I'll find out if I can afford it. If Josh loves it, it could be home.

Day 10 — Today I had my first major depression—the paralyzing variety—in many, many weeks. I haven't had one this bad since I entered treatment.

All day I wrestled with the concepts of loss and resentment and fear, all centered on the fact that I do not own my own home. I am furious with myself for being in this position.

At least somewhere inside of me I know that God is with me, and has a plan and love. And I must keep saying that.

Day 11 — I had an unpleasant meeting with the accountants this morning. Jerry told me I cannot buy the house I went to see. I was very depressed by this financial news. I feel that I have worked so hard and so long for so little security.

Day 12 — Josh is at last his old sweet child-self again, and I am so happy. We are going to take an exotic trip next week even if it is an extravagant thing to do. I want to have time with him alone. We need to grow together.

Day 13 — I made out my will today: chilling, sad, and peculiar. I need to know who my real friends are, and who, besides Josh, really matters. When I am in a better mood I'll have a saner point of view about this: today I feel unglued.

Day 14 — Will I ever, ever have even a flash of sexuality again? Is being sober like being a kind of weirdo vegetarian? Will I ever have any fun? I feel that it has been forever.

Day 15 — I wonder what my future will bring?

I awoke this morning from a dream that I tried to retain. I looked up and saw a serene, handsome man looking lovingly at me, and somehow I knew that he was a poet—the one I have been waiting for.

But of course I have no such man in my life.

What a horrible day this turned out to be! I had a one-and-a-half-hour trip to a local hospital for the Sunday night meeting. I resented leaving my home and my guests, resented the reminder that I have an ongoing problem that needs tending to. But that was nothing compared to the rage I felt when I was trapped in traffic and was an hour late for the meeting.

I am embarrassed to say that I am sick to death of these meetings. I want to spend time with fewer recovering addicts and alcoholics, because all they talk about is themselves and their sickness. I understand why I even might have taken a drink to get through tonight. I wasn't tempted, but I understand the instinct. It is hard.

I long for a social life that is not just about people in recovery. I need more time to meditate and to reflect. I've turned off my phone to see if that will help.

Day 16 — I am taking Josh and his friend Chance to Maui tomorrow. I want to come back a nicer person. I want to dance and be fun and be funny. I am growing too serious, and I don't like the way I feel.

God help me to change, please—and to be happy.

Day 17 — I thought of something while I was in the shower: how is it that there are a number of talented, famous film actresses who seem to have managed to do fine work, for enormous sums of money, and yet live far away from Hollywood, and maintain a long-term relationship with the same man, and have children? I could never do more than two things at one time: maybe actress and mother, or mother and lover, but never all of it at once. And tonight I feel real envy for all the fame and approval and first-class fuss that I haven't really had in ten years. I'm ashamed to admit this, but it's how I feel tonight—unreasonable.

I brought a lot of books to Hawaii, including some

so-called self-help books. God, I had no idea how many ways we could be dysfunctional.

How incomplete it feels not to have a man in this huge resort bed.

I suppose. Romantic ass. Josh and his friend Chance just got back from cruising the beach for beautiful college girls. They are whistling away in the shower, and so happy. I love it. Please don't let him be terrified of intimacy.

Day 19 — I am afraid I've gained weight here, in spite of very little food, and no drink whatsoever. I also have a fever blister, and my foot is bleeding from the fire coral I kicked while I was swimming. I feel like a mess and I am nervous that I won't look glamorous enough next Saturday night when I have agreed to present an Emmy at the Awards. It means a lot to me, especially just now, that "they," the people in the industry whom I perceive to be the Enemy, think I look good. I shall spend the next days being super-careful, so that I can fit into a dress I know looks good on me. No more sugar, bread, mayonnaise, salty olives, or dessert. What a drag. The chocolate-sauced desserts I've eaten for the past three nights have taken the place of wine and a lover. I can't win.

Last night we talked about going home, and that worried me. Where is our home? Where do I begin my life now? I want it to count.

Day 21 — I think of Ben sometimes; I have forgotten what it feels to be sexual. I feel, sometimes, as though the whole treatment experience was a sort of lobotomy— that I cannot feel anything creative anymore.

Who the fuck am I? What do I want to do? Where do I want to go? I am hanging on by my fingernails.

Day 22 — It is our last day here, and I have spent it virtually by myself. I took a 7:00 A.M. walk on that special white sand beach near the hotel, all alone with the crashing turquoise waves and the new day. And now I am still all alone, on my favorite promontory, overlooking two lagoons and the distant emerald fingers of Molokai, crowned with fat rain clouds. I suddenly realize that my terror is all about tomorrow; that today has been just exactly what I have longed for all these months—solitude in a beautiful environment, and the most profound kind of happiness being with my child.

Interlude

Maine, *February 1990*

I t is late afternoon, and the light has just turned very pale pink as the winter sun sets deep in the woods. I have bundled up against the newfound chill and taken the two dogs for a long walk. We followed the trail made several days ago by two cross-country skiers. We left big fuzzy holes where our boots sank into the very wet white that hardened last night with a large drop in temperature. It was ten below zero this morning. The golden retriever, white-faced and wonderful, and the border collie, smiling and hyper, raced on ahead of me. In the stillness of the woods I could hear the jangle of their identification tags. Then they would reappear out of nowhere to "round me up," check on me.

There are one hundred acres of fields and woods and frozen marsh to explore, and in the late winter day you can see for a long, long way. I measured my whereabouts by the distance I felt from the large barn, and I made a loop through the forest until I came to the nearly frozen stream. The retriever dared to cross it; I did not. There were pale icy cuffs along the shallow banks, and even dark swirls of moving water where the stream flowed too fast to freeze. As I wandered through the woods I thought of my childhood. I felt the world stretch out with infinite possibilities, as only a child can know. "I don't know what I want to be when I grow up. I want to be everything." I still do. Nothing has changed. Most of me is still a child, and I find her in the woods.

But there are too many choices and possibilities, and I know that, of course, everything is not possible. I guess I am naïve; it had not occurred to me that I wouldn't be able to have all my dreams.

Or maybe I already have them.

6

JUST TELL ME
WHAT YOU WANT

A little fairy story about a Woman Old Enough to Know Better and a Beautiful Young Man.

Once upon a time in the late nineteen-eighties there was a woman who still believed in romance and in fairy tales and in dreams come true. Time after time she got all dressed up with her best silver bracelets, changed her perfume, filled the house with fresh flowers, and imagined that this time what she heard said by a man would be the real thing. But she had made mistaken choices, time after time. In looking back on the lovely men in her life, she was able to see the hurt she had inflicted by not saying who she really was and what she needed. She regretted her lack of honesty and the lost opportunities for a lasting relationship.

One day she found herself in a New Age bookstore in Los Angeles, searching for answers to some of her bigger questions. As she walked through the aisles of books, she noticed titles like *The Search for Serenity* and *The Tantra of Sex*. Surely somewhere here she would find the answers to her lifelong loneliness and fear. She rolled up the sleeves of her Italian green T-shirt and sat down in the window seat of the cozy bookstore, a stack of books and a basket of quartz crystals by her side. Curious, she leafed through the pages, hoping that some sentence would leap out at her.

Suddenly, from the corner of her eye she noticed a Beautiful Young Man in a red damask shirt and faded blue jeans. He was carrying a motorcycle helmet and studying an assortment of Eastern artifacts in the case next to the window seat. She thought she felt him linger, just a beat long. Could he be looking at her? Sensing her?

Finally he spoke: "Hi."

She replied: "Hi."

"My name is Dan."

She introduced herself and asked, "What do you do, Dan?"

He told her he taught a class called "Be Here Now." Had she heard of it?

The woman shook her head and stared at the Beautiful Young Man. He seemed so calm, so "centered." (Wasn't that the word they were using these days?) She wondered if he might have the answers she was looking for in all the books spread out around her. She asked him if he ever gave private classes, and he told her he did. She agreed to meet him at his office in a week, and she returned to her own home feeling strangely excited. She even dared to wonder, Could he be The One?

The following week she kept her appointment. Even

before the lesson began in "Be Here Now," she knew she would have to tell him what she was feeling, to acknowledge the energy that was by now rushing through her whole being, clouding her concentration and giving a beautiful glow to her face and eyes. Careful to be sure he understood that above all she wanted him to be her teacher, she told him, "I have to clear the air to be able to concentrate and study with you. I need to tell you how very attracted to you I am. And now we can put that aside and go to work. I feel much better and more honest now. It is hard for me to say what I feel because I am so frightened of rejection, but this has been a positive experience for me."

Dan took a deep breath and seemed to be thinking for a minute before he said, "You know, I never go out with my students, but I have to admit that I am attracted to you too."

Each of them having said their little piece, the young man and the woman put their emotions aside, and began to work. He was a good teacher—even a great teacher— and she was a good student who worked very hard. "Be Here Now" made sense to her. She imagined that it might change her life. She would settle for that, and put aside the butterflies she felt when she was in Dan's presence. After all, what was more important? Perhaps the information he had been refining for a decade would help to heal her, to "Open Her Heart," as he described it.

For several weeks the private sessions were so intense that she left his office in tears of frustration. "Don't worry," he said, "you are just finally beginning to Let Go."

She felt encouraged, even proud of his approval and

support. Secretly she longed for this approval. Did he know—did he even think—that she was a Good Person? Did he see that she, too, had been Seeking, although in a different way? She couldn't tell what Dan thought, really, because he was so controlled and removed that, except for his gentleness and his beauty, he showed her none of himself.

One day the telephone rang. It was Dan. He said, "Look, I've been thinking about you, and I realize that there is no good reason why we can't have dinner and see if this electricity we feel isn't about something real."

It was raining the night of their dinner, and the woman was so nervous about their meeting that she was afraid she would crash her car. They both toyed with their pasta pomodoro basilica, and talked about nothing. The air grew more and more charged with the tension of their attraction to each other.

Finally Dan said to her: "Take a deep breath—slow down. Let's just Be Here Now." And he kissed her very lightly on the lips as they parted outside the restaurant.

The light rain continued, and the woman drove home slowly, as if in a trance, all the dark way up the coast to her house and her animals.

Uh-oh, she was falling in love.

The events of the next few weeks passed by in a blur. She continued to work very hard in her class, longing to get an A in the final exam, and hoping against hope that she might be the woman for him.

And suddenly, she was.

What a love affair they had! "Be Here Now" indeed! Had she ever felt so Present, so Connected, so happy? For once in her life the woman was not even drinking champagne to celebrate, and she laughed out loud to herself every morning when she woke up and realized how happy she was. Although she continued to take her private classes very seriously and very professionally, she had a glow that only comes·with love. And so did he. He told her he had never been so happy in all his young life, that she was everything he ever dreamed of, that together they could and would have everything.

Piece by piece he moved himself into her house. First came his compact disc of the Fine Young Cannibals, and next came his macrobiotic cookbook and the red damask shirt. One day he brought his two enormous gray Irish wolfhounds with their dinner bowls—their names, Om and Shanti, painted on the sides. The family was here to stay.

For richer, for poorer, in sickness and in health.

The woman couldn't believe her life. Finally, finally, a man who would and did love her real self, for once and forever. Slowly, with his support, she began to peel away her layers of distrust. To her amazement she found she could give up her independence and solitude and imagine living with someone: him. She rearranged the closets, she rearranged the rooms, and she looked the other way when the younger of the wolfhounds bit one of her cats, sending him out into the coyote-ridden canyon in terror. If this was Being Here Now, then surely everyone in their blissful little family would adjust, sooner or later, and very peacefully.

The woman and the Beautiful Young Man took long walks with their dogs, and spent hours preparing special canine meals from recipes donated by their mutual nutritionist. As they steamed the brown rice and sautéed the tofu and shredded the daikon, they fairly beamed with Inner Light, imagining all the love that was going into their dogs' dinners. For themselves they went to spas in search of sulfurous water strong enough to complete their purification and bring them even closer to Being Here Now.

For the Woman Old Enough to Know Better, life began to feel like ecstasy. For the young man it held promise, but he still preferred to rise an hour before dawn each morning and retreat to his private study (the one she had created out of her former garage) to work on his Ph.D. thesis. Every morning the woman would wake up and stretch to touch the Beautiful Young Man, only to find him already gone. Saddened, she took to preparing him large bowls of fresh papayas and mangos and New Zealand strawberries as a sort of apology for her still primitive erotic needs. She was pleased when he said "Thank you," and she worked even harder that week.

God, how she longed to Be Here Now.

They took exotic trips. Once, on a day's notice, they flew to Budapest to stay in a pink and gilt room, and they spent their days in the parks and their nights at the opera. Another time they went to a resort in Costa Rica. When the woman was offered a short job in New York, with tickets for both of them, they spent their time with a number of his friends who had already completed their theses in Be Here Now.

For one weekend they shared a small house with eight grown-ups, five children, a baby, two dogs, a parakeet, several goldfish, and four cats. It was wonderful and inspiring. The woman saw firsthand what it was like to Be Here Now, and although she knew she didn't quite fit in yet, she did her part, scraping raw summer corn from the cobs, and stirring it into the kale purée. She knew it was only a matter of time before she, too, would renounce caffeine and privacy and learn to Be Here Now.

At last she stopped expressing her loneliness when the Beautiful Young Man chose to remain in the swimming pool on his inflated dinosaur, or talk for hours about the subject they were studying. She was learning just how much further she had to go before she would be considered Real and Worthy, and she vowed to study even harder. After all, she loved the young man so much. She longed to see the veil of sadness lift from his beautiful face, and moreover, she longed to be the reason for him, too, to let down his formidable barriers.

Holidays came and went, a rainbow of love and celebration, hopes and dreams for the future. The Woman Old Enough to Know Better and the Beautiful Young Man began to behave like a couple. It was thrilling; it was terrifying; it was happening.

They had just come back from a magical vacation together. A friend had offered the use of his family's old ranch in Sedona, Arizona, and they were going to take him up on it. They talked about trying it out for a year, a sort of adventure together.

Dan had said, "But how do I make a living in Sedona?"

And the Woman Old Enough to Know Better had said, "Oh, darling, it's obvious. Just do your brilliant seminars in Be Here Now." And so it was settled.

Now that they were home the woman had an unsettling thought: in order for her to concentrate fully on her own thesis on Being Here Now and to earn the A she so desperately craved from Dan, she would have to go into seclusion for a month. She dreaded the separation from her loved one, but inasmuch as her teacher was inordinately disciplined in his own studies, she knew he would understand. So she packed up her textbooks, some woolen socks, twelve photographs of her Beautiful Young Man, and tearfully kissed him *à bientôt*. Dan returned the kiss ever so lightly and wished her good luck on her thesis, adding: "Hurry home."

On the plane to northern Minnesota and the cabin where she would write her final paper, the woman experienced a fleeting anxiety. Why had the Beautiful Young Man forfeited dinner with her on their last night together, choosing instead to drive a twenty-one-year-old model friend from the Los Angeles airport to Oxnard?

The Woman Old Enough to Know Better shook her head sadly and dared to wonder if perhaps her Dan was getting a little tired of her. "Hmmm," she thought, as she placed a tiny capsule of oscillococcinum under her tongue, hoping to ward off the flu she felt coming on. "Don't be silly. We're on our way to a New Life Together once this month is over! Chin up!"

The woman spent a month in hell. She wrote and wrote and wrote about the past, hoping to put it behind her once and for all, so that she could truly Be Here Now. With him. And with an A on her paper.

As she had no telephone in her cabin, she had made plans to talk to Dan only twice during her self-imposed exile. She would walk the eight miles through the snow-encrusted forest, finding her way to the shack that was both a House of Pancakes and a Whole Earth Catalogue outlet, as well as the Chevron station and local veterinary clinic. There, huddled in an outdoor phone booth, she would leave her lovesick messages for Dan. On his machine. After all, he had a demanding teaching schedule.

In return, she received two beautiful, beautiful letters. Both mentioned the Bond they had, the Void without her, the yearning for their life to begin together, the dreams, the aches, the sheer loneliness of life without the Woman Who Should Have Known Better. Her heart warmed. Surely, when this month in hell was over, she would return to his open arms, and they would soon be in Sedona with his school and Om and Shanti and her own dogs and cats and furniture, and their special dream. It was all too exciting, too brave, too wonderful.

The day finally came for her to pack up her book bag with her finished thesis. She was once again a teenager in love as she anticipated the reunion they would have and the path they would soon begin. At the airport she bought him a beautiful necklace of extra-powerful quartz crystals. She traveled all day, and at the two airports where she had to wait to change planes, she saw that she looked exhausted from her hard month's work. "Some good macrobiotic food would do me a world of good," she mused. Maybe they could spend their first night together in a health spa.

When she arrived in Los Angeles and looked toward the waiting area, her heart soared. "Dan!" she cried. "Oh, my beautiful, beautiful Dan!"

He held her tenderly, and shyly presented her with an enormous bouquet of orange tiger lilies. "Shanti ran your cat off three weeks ago, and I can't find him anywhere," he said. "And Om put four hundred and fifty dollars' worth of emergency stitches into your dog's face, darling."

"Fuck the dogs," said the woman to her Beautiful Young Man. "The important thing is us. Let's just you and I Be Here Now."

But as they waited for her luggage to arrive, there was a chilling, terrible pause. The woman was so attuned to Dan that she asked, "Is something the matter, darling?"

He looked pained and heavy, and slowly he replied, not looking into her eyes.

"I have just spent a few days with an old school friend and all of that time I have been watching his young wife and their infant son. It is all so wonderful and so moving and so important to me. I feel this strong bond growing in me. Call it family—call it what you will— but it is Calling Me."

The Woman Old Enough to Know Better looked at him and said, "When do you want to have children, Dan?"

And he replied, "In three years. Maybe five."

"But what about *Now*?" she cried. "What does it mean to you, *Now*? When you wrote me that valentine last week, did you feel this way? What does all this have to do with three years from *Now*? I just don't understand."

She was crying now, and waving the tiger lilies about wildly, covering the airport security men and their dogs with fine yellow powder from the stamens of the flowers. The dogs, confusing it with some exotic cocaine, grew mad with excitement. They jumped all over her, barking loudly and tearing her Giorgio Armani jacket with their teeth until one of the security men raised his hand and shouted, "Shut up, Wolf! That's tiger lily dust, not coke, you dumb asshole!"

And the woman, still sobbing, said, "Darling, whatever happened to Be Here Now? I'm finally, finally really here, and now you're pulling away from me, breaking my heart, shattering my dreams. Oh, please, Dan, please."

But the Beautiful Young Man seemed to retreat into himself before her very eyes. She thought of that day so long ago when she, dressed in black tights and an Italian green T-shirt, had first spotted Dan from her corner in the bookstore. Now he had the same heavy, sad, fear-laden look in his eyes. She knew she was losing him, and she was devastated.

He said, "I'm sorry. I don't want to hurt you. You have given me the happiest year of my life, but I have to prepare for three years from now. I just can't Be Here Now."

One week later, while she was in Arizona undoing all the plans they had made for the future, he came to her house and took away: his brown-rice cooker, his red damask shirt, two reggae discs and the Fine Young Cannibals, two Versace jackets, and *The Search for Serenity* and *The Tantra of Sex*. He also took Om, Shanti, their bowls, and their Christmas leashes. He left on her desk his corrected copy of her thesis, "Be Here Now."

She sat down at her desk and looked at the photographs of her and the Beautiful Young Man. And one by one she removed them from their silver frames. She put them all away in a large manila envelope, hoping to speed away the pain of memory. "No question about it," she sighed. "We did look happy together." Lost in thought and munching on her fourth Häagen-Dazs bar, she happened to look out of her window just in time to see her big white cat come creeping around the corner, peering cautiously for the wolfhounds. He was home at last, safe and sound. He was a sign from God that all was once again right with her world. She picked up her thesis one last time. "A" he had written in red Magic Marker on the top right-hand corner. "Be Here Now." She took a green marker, and with a sad smile, the Woman Old Enough to Know Better added: "Thank you for that class—God, was it hard."

7

FADE-IN

An important part of my ongoing recovery has been to clean up with the people I harmed along the way. I am still making these amends, such is the litter of my past. Sometimes it is easy, the person in question being understanding and supportive; sometimes they just do not know what I am talking about. Perhaps there will even be a few who will not forgive me, but I have not run into them yet.

Making amends is a powerful experience. It involves taking a cold, hard look at my behavior toward other people all these years, and then taking full responsibility for everything I have said and done. It is often painful, even shaming. It is absolutely necessary in the great garbage-cleaning process called recovery.

One day I was thinking about my list of amends and the word itself started to look funny, the way words do when you look at them over and over again. As my eyes tried to make sense of this suddenly peculiar jumble of letters, I realized that the word *amends* can be a fantastic anagram for me—that scrambled inside it are many words key to my life, and to me, Ali MacGraw (A.M.). For fun, I sat down and tried to find them all, particularly the important ones.

AM

My part of the verb *to be*. Powerful and present
for my own life.

ME

Time to come clean about who that is, so that
the next fifty years will be easier
and more authentic.

MEN

Oh, boy! This is a basket of serpents; trouble and
confusion and misplaced trust and dreams. Also
the victims of my dysfunctional behavior.

NAME

From the very beginning I wanted to have a
completely different name for my Screen Actors
Guild credits, partly to protect my critical
parents' privacy, and partly to protect my own. I
never could settle on one that seemed to fit, and
besides, no one ever came up with "Lani Wolff
. . . in *Goodbye, Columbus*"!

SANE

The opposite of insane, which I was afraid I was
becoming at one point. I was not, but my life was
definitely out of control.
Now I have taken charge.
I am sane.
Surprise!

SAM

Peckinpah. I did *The Getaway* and *Convoy* with
him, always grateful that I was one of his few
female friends and not a hapless lover of this
quintessential male-chauvinist artist-cowboy.
I miss him.

MEAN

I can be mean. And I don't want to be anymore.
And I want to say what I mean . . .
(another meaning).

AD(S)

I did some of these, as a model, on my way to
becoming a movie star: a little larva hatched into
a perfectly made-up, coiffed, dressed,
and pinned butterfly.
Always a stranger to her own body.

DAN

As time goes by and the pain subsides, I can
focus on the good things he gave me.

Sea and sand

The beach in Malibu where I lived for over
fifteen years. Walks at sunrise and sunset were a
form of meditation. The beach, a tonic.

Mend(s)

Repairs. They are much needed: my heart, my
trust, my huge ego—and other people I have
stamped on with cleats.

End(s)

"Tie them all up": some behavior has to be
acknowledged and owned and finished.
I am ready for new beginnings.

Amen

Hallelujah!

Lincoln's Birthday, 1990. It is twilight now. The sun has just set behind the winter woods, leaving trails of palest orange and turquoise—a Tiepolo painting. I took the dogs out with me—or rather, they took me with them. A great deal of snow melted this weekend, and there are patches everywhere of mashed-down grazing grass and even sweet-smelling hay. The earth smells ready for spring, but winter hasn't done with it yet. We made our way to a little valley filled with flat-needled spruce and small beech trees with chamois-colored leaves. Here there are huge old trees whose trunks and limbs have been split by some terrible storm. On the deciduous trees grow every imaginable moss and lichen—a kingdom of Chinese-green ruffles, with an occasional wild mushroom like a child's flying-saucer-shaped ice-cream sandwich. On a few bushes, dried leaves and chocolate-colored pods remain, still and frozen.

Best is the stream, caught between freezing and rushing on into springtime. Last week it disappeared under a thick hat of opalescent ice so strong that the dogs and I marched across it quite safely, but now it is so fragile and lacelike that the littlest twig falling on it shatters the crystalline surface. Over and over again I stop to stare at the patterns of the ice, melting and freezing and melting again, right before my eyes. In one spot a huge old rotting birch has fallen across the stream, and where the log touches the water with its little birch whiskers, large Christmas bells of ice have formed, anchoring the tree to the stream below. In another place the water rushes in great circular motions, freezing in ovals as it touches the snowy bank. In some places the ice is black and transparent, so that you can see the inky leaves on the stream's bottom. And in others it is opaque gray, disguising its thinness. Only the telltale musical sound of the brook gives away the news that it is building up its strength for spring.

I cannot help wondering about the future of these woods. What are we doing to our planet? How long can our earth endure the battering we have given it in the twentieth century? Nothing is sacred if money and power are in control, not even our land and air and oceans. The northern forests are destroyed by acid rain from the cities, and the Amazon rain forest decimated so that more cattle can be force-fed to produce more hamburgers. More nuclear bombs are detonated under the earth's surface, just to be sure they still "work." And millions of tons of surplus food lie rotting in depots of starving countries, while politicians bicker over whether or not to distribute it.

Even in the microcosm of my old home, Malibu, there has been an ongoing battle over a proposed plan for waste disposal. I remember the shock we all felt when the politicians countered our fears about the inevitable pollution of the public beaches and the whole Pacific Ocean. They offered their solution: "stream enhancement." What? An astonishing choice of words to describe dumping raw sewage into the mountain streams, which would eventually carry it out to sea. As I contemplate the purity of this little stream in the Maine woods, I am filled with frustration and rage at the obliviousness of so many powerful people in our time. Don't they know that the clock is running out?

I have an uneasiness tonight about my future, as a result of these twelve days I have spent in this little town, Belfast. I have met so many nice people here—the exercise teachers and the dry cleaner, salespeople from the art and office-supply stores, the florist, the owner of the local coffee shop, and more. I feel welcome.

And then there is life in my company town, Hollywood. My heart breaks for every man who is running a studio or talent agency, because he knows that if he gets up from lunch to go to the men's room, somebody will be in his chair when he returns. And if he spends too much time in a loving relationship with his family instead of discussing with his boss just who got the vice-presidential chair at Disney, he is done for. Maybe this exists in Washington and Detroit as well, and maybe it exists in Hong Kong. I don't know. But in Hollywood, a man is defined by Is He Hot?

It is disturbing to sit here in Maine, alone in front of my fire, while the day tries to summon up more snow outside my window, and I contemplate the future. I cannot escape some kind of deep discomfort within me—the feeling that I belong here, or in a facsimile of here, at least some of the time. How to do this?

Today, on my walk, I had my longest thoughts to date about drinking. The snow was coming down in huge flakes, and the old farmhouse and barn looked like a Christmas card. Everything was white and shades of gray, except for the lace-covered pine trees. It was achingly beautiful. I know what I would have done three and a half years ago. I would have come back from my walk, done my chores, and then started to drink. On a day like today it might have been cognac, something powerful, to "warm" me. Or I might have grabbed a goblet of red wine, with the excuse of needing a cozy glow. I even felt some anxiety that I might actually *do* it today. But I didn't.

Here in Maine, alone and quiet, I am in touch with a kind of sanity I have been missing. I need silence in which to absorb the colors of twilight—the mauve shadows of the trees at sunset, and the great clusters of smoky clouds as they gather overhead. I need stillness to appreciate the curls of woodsmoke as they come out of the central chimney. And I need time to note each separate layer of color in the moss-agate landscape of pine and birch.

And when I have done that, I feel centered again. The big challenge will be how to duplicate the serenity I find here when I am in an environment that lacks the nourishment of this one.

·   ·   ·

THIS AFTERNOON the local veterinarian, who spends most of his day out in the country, invited me to accompany him on his rounds. I adore all animals, and I guess I would rescue and keep every stray dog in the world if I could. But the last time someone invited me on an animal outing, it turned out to be less about the creatures than about their so-called masters. Someone asked me if I would award the Best in Show trophy at the Santa Monica Dog Show. I thought it sounded like fun. I had never been to a dog show, but I knew they were pretty serious business. I also knew that, according to old covers of *The New Yorker,* all dogs look like their owners. (My only previous moment of dog-fame came years ago, in 1962, when Melvin Sokolsky put me on a huge wooden crate containing two champion Newfoundlands he had bred and was sending abroad as a gift to the Prince of Morocco. I was a handy prop for the photograph: long straight hair, black leotard, and miniskirt, sitting on the crates, which read PROPERTY OF THE KING OF MOROCCO. It became one of my first magazine covers: *Dog World.* Ah, fame.)

On the morning of the show, I put on some clean jeans and a nice shirt, rather pretty shoes and some silver jewelry—what I thought was an appropriate costume as the celebrity award-giver. As I drove down Santa Monica Boulevard with a friend, I was stunned to see a huge banner strung across all four lanes at the busiest section of the street proclaiming: SANTA MONICA DOG SHOW! WITH ALI MACGRAW! I arrived at the show and had a wonderful time watching all the obsessed dog owners yank their creatures and cajole them into standing still, or walking in the "correct" way—whatever it was that the dogs themselves didn't want to do at that particular moment.

As the afternoon wore on, a woman about my age approached me with a rather angry and disgusted expression. "Is that what you're going to look like?" she asked rudely.

I didn't know what she was talking about until she added, "Did you bring something else to wear when you present the trophy?"

Of course I hadn't, and besides, I thought I looked pretty good for a bunch of animals, no matter how pedigreed. To my horror I heard myself suggest that perhaps there would be time for me to drive the forty minutes back to my house to change. Anything to please. But suddenly she had a burst of face-saving largess and, sizing me up, decided we were enough alike that I could change into her entire outfit, Henri Bendel dress, shoes, stockings, and all. I thanked her, but—no, thank you.

I contemplated leaving, but someone told me that she was in the middle of a falling-out with some other dog-fanatic official. I gave out the trophy, sensing her glaring at me from across the ring, and went home the wiser for dog-show etiquette and uniform.

The next year as I was driving down Santa Monica Boulevard, there it was again: the same banner proclaiming SANTA MONICA DOG SHOW! WITH ALI MACGRAW! I told my publicist to call the AKC and tell them that if the sign was not removed by the next day, I was going to come in and let all the dogs out of their little cages. In my wrong outfit.

The afternoon with George Holmes, the vet, promised to be a different sort of experience, I contemplated canceling when he called up to say he'd be by to pick me up just as soon as he finished packing his surgical instruments.

We set out to visit several dairy farms, where he had "patients," and I watched him work an everyday miracle on one of them—an operation on a cow's fourth stomach. (I didn't know they had more than one.) We were met by a shiny black Labrador puppy and a young boy with red cheeks and a big smile and a cart of wood chips, which he was spreading on the barn floor. They led us to the boy's father, a fourth-generation dairy farmer. He plays country-and-western guitar several nights a month. Otherwise, he minds his big dairy from five o'clock in the morning until eight at night, 365 days of the year. He had one weekend off two summers ago, to go to a livestock auction out of state. And he went to a wedding in New Hampshire a few years back.

THE VET tapped the stomach of the forlorn-looking cow, whose name was Jody, and invited me to listen to the particular resonance that indicated her stomach was turned upside down. Then he told me to feel her ears. They were cold. That meant she was sick. Mine were cold, too, but I was not sick: just awe-struck by the amount of life-and-death work surrounding the deceptively pastoral life of a dairy farmer.

I watched as Jody was led into a big stall, where special care had been taken to clear the floor of dirt.

The operation itself was astonishing. The men tied poor Jody by her front and back ankles, easily forcing her down to the floor on her side. Then they rolled her over on her back and lashed her to the adjacent stalls. Cows don't sleep on their backs, and Jody was terrified. What must she have been thinking as her stomach was swabbed with disinfectant and locally anesthetized by a dozen or more pokes of a big needle? The tremendous Holstein bull eyed her from his adjacent stall, but most of the time he just ate the extra food he had been given to keep him from roaring during the operation.

The vet unrolled his package of instruments and set them on some sterilized cloth, which he had spread out on a milking stool. He worked very fast because he was afraid that Jody, now pretty stoned, might choke to death on her own vomit. Gently he slit layer after layer of her hide and flesh with his surgical knife, stopping only to tie off blood vessels, and to mop the blood with big gauze patches. Finally he reached into the cavity with a plastic-gloved hand and turned the stomach back over. The farmer handed him sutures one by one, from sterilized packs, and in a very few minutes it was all done. The creature was untied and helped to her feet, wobbly for an instant. Then, promptly, as though nothing particularly out of the ordinary had happened, she proceeded to devour her dinner.

I felt that I had been present at a miracle. For a moment there, in the light of the swinging, clip-on bulb, it was as if I were an observer at the Manger.

My own world seemed suddenly very shallow. How preposterous the salaries of movie stars for three months of work, compared to the earnings of a whole farming family, all working around the clock, day after day, year in, year out. I was grateful to have been invited to go on this doctor's rounds: I needed to be reminded of reality.

. . .

THE WHOLE two-decade experience of Hollywood and stardom has been dizzying. For many years I have protested at the top of my lungs that I am not spoiled, that I am not materialistic, that I am still a simple creature from Bedford Village, New York, with my New England rules and morality. Over and over I have proclaimed that no matter what happens in this carnival called stardom, I can always go back to being a waitress or a chambermaid—careers I perfected long ago, during school breaks.

I think I made all those little speeches in a desperate attempt to hang on to some sense of the familiar, because once *Goodbye, Columbus* was released and reviewed, I knew I was in way over my head. I made superior remarks about people who get carried away with the impossibly glittery trappings of celebrity, and I realize today with some embarrassment that those remarks were often born of envy and insecurity.

I have had the most astonishing fuss made over me for twenty years—applause and approval, presents and trips, lavish hotel rooms and first-class everything.

And I have become used to those perks, I am afraid. Yes, I love beautiful things, and I have learned that it is okay to admit to being proud of certain accomplishments, and to show delight at some of the goodies that have come my way (rather than pretend, as I used to, that they didn't mean anything, that I didn't deserve them). I *want* all the goodies: the respect, and the work opportunities, and the lazy days in Venice and the velvety nights in Bali, the beautiful muck-green Armani jacket and the Tibetan turquoise amulet. All that. In addition to passion with a man who really gets who I am—because I dare to show him—and love and mischief and adventure with those astonishing creatures, men and women, who are my friends.

However, these past few years of difficulty finding work and the waning of my stardom have provided me with invaluable lessons. I have learned from the lean times that there is absolutely nothing as paralyzing as a warped reverie about the past or some projected terror of the future. Slowly I am learning that as long as I stay focused on the right-now, I am fine.

During the last few years I have had no serious offers to do either films or television. At first it scared me and bashed my ego around, but nowadays I care only about doing a serious, good piece of work in a film before I make my exit from this scene. I have paid considerable dues, and the best of my work speaks for itself. So it was with a rather wry smile that I recently heard an agent tell me, in his third phone call since he decided to represent me, that a producer-whose-movie-might-get-made wanted to meet me for the title part, and I should immediately plan to have lunch with him to discuss it. The film was to be called . . . *Talk Dirty!*

I told the agent that, before we wasted our time, I would like to see a script. He said that no one was happy with the script yet, and so they wanted to tell me the story themselves at lunch.

I didn't want to hear it. I have, on the average, three people a week tell me their ideas about the great films they want to make—usually in the checkout line in the supermarket. The agent then said, conspiratorially, that he would try to "sneak a copy" for me, which made me furious. I told him that as I had been doing this for eighteen years now, I felt totally comfortable just asking to read a script—no stupid nonsense about sneaking it. He was reluctant, but he found the script and immediately sent it over for me to read.

The first page was pretty routine. The leading lady was quickly described as being a Grown-Up—a "very creative person" who smokes constantly and is always busy doing her side job, which is, of course, talking dirty on the phone. I don't remember the deathless opening prose, but it was something like "Hi! (breath). Do you have your dick out?"

I slogged through it, page after endless page, experiencing a kind of wonder that my career had culminated in this dazzling moment. Imagine! I was being considered to play this artsy, impoverished (I guess) woman who supported her Greenwich Village life style with telephone sex. Oh, well, a leading lady has to make a living. Maybe it would take a turn for the incandescent and become *Son of Klute*.

I read on: the woman overhears a murder during one of her sleazy phone calls, and she proceeds for the rest of the film to try to solve the murder with the help of a policeman and her little sister, whose role in the film was to be "steamy" and not much more.

Finally, I reached the dramatic and thrilling confrontation between the Nazi psycho murderer and me: "You and I are alike, bitch," he screams. "Look at you! Two hundred and fifty pounds! I'll bet you haven't had sex in eight years. We're the same, you and I. Who's the sick one here?"

I called the agent and asked him if he had read the

script, and of course he hadn't. When I told him what sort of character they were sending me up for, the agent smoothly advised me, "They will change all that."

That was a little like saying that a reduction in finger sandwiches at White House receptions would fix the national debt. If this movie were *Raging Bull II,* I wouldn't grow Robert De Niro's stomach for the profile in front of the television, so 250 pounds was pretty much out of the question, even for Art. I told the agent that *Talk Dirty* would certainly qualify as the final nail in my coffin, so if they wanted to exploit the girl from *Love Story* one more time, it would cost them a minimum of $20 million. As far as I know that was the hang-up, dial tone, and disconnect for *Talk Dirty* on the Hollywood circuit. Sorry, wrong number.

I have learned important new words in these classroom days—and none more important than the word *authentic*. At long last I have come to realize that none of us has anything more valuable to offer than who we *really* are.

It's easy to look at someone like me and assume that all the shiny details add up to a whole person, one whose life and feelings have always been in perfect order. But underneath the movie magazine superficialities of clothes and prizes, the tabloid-fodder marriages, there beats an ordinary human heart. I am learning—oh, so slowly— that I need to be comfortable with myself, without the approval of others as some measure of personhood. I have a right to expect honesty and vulnerability from my friends, as they do from me. I am learning that my lifelong habit of doctoring my presentation of myself to others is nothing more than another version of my need to control, to do everything—even friendship—my way. It has not made me happy, and the time has come for me to change.

I can and I am: it is exciting work, brand-new territory. As I feel myself growing, I feel my life changing, and in no area has it been more evident than in the area of fear.

Fear has been my companion—my enemy, actually— but so close to me that it has not occurred to me to send it away, until recently. Fear came to Rosemary Hall with me, and then to Wellesley. Fear came to all my weddings, and often to work, even before the movies. Fear sneaked up beside me when I strutted through my first screen test for *The President's Analyst,* and moved in forever right after *Goodbye, Columbus* was released. Fear winks at me from the lenses of the cameras, both still and motion picture, that have photographed me. And fear has haunted me for hours and days about my clothes and haircuts and basic presentability at every industry func- tion. About the only times fear has declined to accompany me have been in the raising of my son, or in the presence of my animals, or for the wrapping of Christmas presents.

Or for the 1989 Academy Awards ceremony.

Twenty years before, at the Oscar show, I was a pre- senter of the award for something like Best Screenplay Adapted from Another Medium. The category was filled with unpronounceable names, and I was grateful that my partner, James Earl Jones, drew most of them to read off the teleprompter. At the afternoon rehearsal there were various luminaries from the Academy of Motion Picture Arts and Sciences, the big voters, all of whom seemed to be sitting in the front row, talking incessantly and loudly amongst themselves. As I came onstage, one of the old geezers said, in a loud voice, "Who is that, anyway? Elliott Gould?"

For months I had been petrified at the thought of participating once again in the Oscar show, this one arranged by an old supporter, Allan Carr. As the weeks sped by and I read that over a billion people would be watching, I became more and more terrified. I was sure everyone would wonder why I was even up there, since I hadn't done a film or television show in at least three years. Who did I think I was? A movie star? Why? Ali who? I thought about all the ravishing women who were going to be onstage that night, their portfolios filled with recent rave press clippings, and many of their bodies remodeled to perfection.

But something incredible had happened without my realizing it: José Eber had given me a great new haircut, and Giorgio Armani had given me a beautiful dress—these things help, of course. And I had spent several hours doing a yoga meditation to quiet my anxious heart. By the time I actually stepped on that stage in front of God-knows-how-many people all over the world, I felt an unexpected surge of confidence and calm. Suddenly I understood that Ali MacGraw was indeed not the center of the universe, and that this microscopic moment could be fun and easy. By the time I was called to do my twenty-seven-second appearance on the show, I was so relaxed that I knew it would go well. So, of the many years between that first, panic-filled appearance on the telecast and the last one, I draw one conclusion: I own what I am and do, and I no longer need to depend on the kindness of strangers in order to feel confident. At long last I am beginning to feel comfortable that I am wearing the right costume—my own skin. If I am ever asked to do it again, I know fear will not be onstage with me. Miracle.

When I began this book several years ago I thought that I could perhaps tie everything up in the end with a tidy little paragraph about the Work, the Man, the Permanent Home, the Answer for the Future. But surprise—I cannot. Not like in the movies: more like real life. I even have come to realize that I wouldn't want it to conclude neatly with THE END. Certainly not now, not at the new beginning of my life.

Today, like the child I remember as I walk in the Maine woods, I see *everything* as possible. If I remain authentic. Progress still feels like six steps forward and five steps back, an exasperating amount of hard work to gain that little inch. And I still have days of sadness and nameless fear, but never, as before, black despair. I really believe I have been inordinately blessed, and that God is not giving me one bit more than I can handle. And if ever I am foolish enough to question His existence in my life, I have only to look at the dazzling proof of this love in the constant caring of my friends.

I have learned a number of difficult lessons the hard way, because I guess I was always so sure that I had a better plan. It is time for some humility, and for the realization that after all this time I really know very little about anything.

Every single new discovery is a gift and an opportunity, an often disguised blessing and an adventure. It is a mesmerizing, slowly unfolding process—moving pictures.

POSTSCRIPT

Dearest Josh,

I am sitting in front of a log fire in this cozy farmhouse in Maine. Outside it is cold, damp New England winter—fresh snow on the branches, and more on the way. I have done all the chores: filled the tall plastic bird feeder with black sunflower seeds from the metal container in the garage, fed the two dogs, one of whom is now asleep on the floor next to me by the fire. I have coaxed the little red cat to eat, in spite of the fact that she isn't feeling too well. I have sprayed the fuzzy leaves of the pink geranium with water, and have filled the fireplace basket with wood, which I brought from the ceiling-high stacks in the cellar. All is in order now. It is peaceful here. I think it is the only

place I could ever have written my book, which is
finally, above all, for you.

You never knew my parents well enough to understand just why this environment is so important to me.
In our lifetime together we have been fortunate to live
rather luxuriously. Because of my glittery job and celebrity, we have traveled exotically, and have enjoyed
treats and adventures and attentions that were very
nice.

But a small part of my heart is deeply rooted in
New England winter, when it is so silent that you can
hear the snowflakes as they fall in the woods. I have the
time and space to reflect here, to be alone without feeling
lonely, to go back over my life as I begin the second
half, and search for lessons learned and ways to do it
better this time around. It is a privileged moment in
my life, and I treasure every second of it. What I want
to see emerge from this is a clear picture of who I am,
and where I have been, and what I have learned—for
me, and for you. I hope that when you read this, you
will find areas of my life to celebrate, as well as to
forgive. I hope you will respect my search, and maybe
even save yourself from some of my terrible mistakes.
I hope you will better know who I am, understand me,
and even yourself, a little better. I hope this book will
help you, as writing it has helped me.

From the very instant that I saw your big/little feet
poking out from the basket in my room in the hospital
on January 16, 1971, I have valued and respected and
loved you unconditionally. With all of the fabulous
adventures I have had in this first half of my life, it

has been our friendship and trust that have been the biggest gift. And so, here is this book—my thank-you gift to you.

I love you.

Yo' Mama
Belfast, Maine
February 1990

DON'T MISS YOUR FAVORITE
MOVIES IN PRINT!

- ❑ **BONFIRE OF THE VANITIES,** Tom Wolfe 27597-6 $5.95
- ❑ **THE RUSSIA HOUSE,** John LeCarre 28534-3 $5.95
- ❑ **THE LITTLE DRUMMER GIRL,**
  John LeCarre 26757-4 $5.95
- ❑ **AN INCONVENIENT WOMAN,**
  Dominick Dunne 28906-3 $5.99
- ❑ **PEOPLE LIKE US,** Dominick Dunne 27891-6 $5.95
- ❑ **DICK TRACY,** Max Allan Collins 28528-9 $4.95
- ❑ **HAMLET,** William Shakespeare 21292-3 $2.95
- ❑ **THE TERMINATOR,** Frakes and Wisher 25317-4 $4.99
- ❑ **TERMINATOR 2: JUDGEMENT DAY,**
  Randall Frakes 29169-6 $4.99
- ❑ **CONAGHER,** Louis L'Amour 28101-1 $3.99
- ❑ **VOICE OF THE HEART,**
  Barbara Taylor Bradford 26253-X $5.95
- ❑ **WHITE PALACE,** Glenn Savan 27659-X $4.95
- ❑ **SOPHIE'S CHOICE,** William Styron 27749-9 $5.95
- ❑ **CALL OF THE WILD/WHITE FANG,**
  Jack London 21233-8 $2.95
- ❑ **THE BOURNE IDENTITY,** Robert Ludlum ... 26011-1 $5.95
- ❑ **LOVE STORY,** Erich Segal 27528-3 $4.95
- ❑ **THE PRINCE OF TIDES,** Pat Conroy 26888-0 $5.99
- ❑ **BALLAD OF THE SAD CAFE,**
  Carson McCullers 27254-3 $3.95

Available at your local bookstore or use this page to order.
Send to: Bantam Books, Dept.   NFB 2
        2451 S. Wolf Road
        Des Plaines, IL 60018
Please send me the items I have checked above. I am enclosing
$_____ (please add $2.50 to cover postage and handling). Prices
are $1.00 higher per book in Canada. Send check or money order, no cash
or C.O.D.'s, please.

Mr/Ms._____

Address_____

City/State_____Zip_____
Please allow four to six weeks for delivery.
Prices and availability subject to change without notice.   NFB 2 3/92

Don't miss the real stories behind these top celebrities

A DAMNED SERIOUS BUSINESS
by Rex Harrison
The king of comedy reveals the secrets behind his success in a warm and wonderfully humorous memoir completed shortly before his death.

❑ 07341-9 $21.95/26.95 in Canada

CALL ME ANNA: The Autobiography of Patty Duke
by Patty Duke and Kenneth Turan
The youngest actor ever to win an Oscar reveals her turbulent life and the discovery of the long-hidden illness that led to her amazing recovery.

❑ 27205-5 $5.99/6.99 in Canada

MOVING PICTURES: An Autobiography
by Ali MacGraw
Wry, witty, and refreshingly frank, Ali MacGraw discloses the truth behind the myth, the marriages, and the Hollywood hype.

❑ 29551-9 $5.99/$6.99 in Canada

ALL HIS JAZZ: The Life and Death of Bob Fosse
by Martin Gottfried
The candid details, the backstage dramas, the Dexedrine highs, and the romantic lows—of the razzle-dazzle life of this dynamic, controversial, thoroughly intriguing artist.

❑ 07038-X $24.95/$29.95 in Canada

DANCE WHILE YOU CAN
by Shirley MacLaine
Illustrated with 32 pages of personal family photos, here is a rich, revealing look at a woman in the prime of her life and at the height of her powers as an artist.

❑ 07607-8 $22.50/$27.50 in Canada